David Rowand

PAISLEY

David Rowand

Fellow, University of Paisley. F.S.A. Scot

David Rowand's Paisley © David Rowand 2001

First published in 2001 by
PASLET PUBLICATIONS,
8a Calside Avenue, Paisley,
Scotland, PA2 6DD.
E-mail:paslet@hotmail.com

Printed in Scotland by Bell & Bain Ltd, Glasgow.
Design & Layout by Chris Rowand & Nicola Brown.
ISBN No.0 9539599 1 0
British Library Cataloguing in Publication Data.
A CIP record for this book is available from the British Library.

Introduction

'David Rowand's Paisley' is the sequel to the highly successful 'Silver Threads' and is the author's fourth book written about the town of his birth. The fully illustrated book aims to share scenes of Paisley's colourful past.

Telling stories to Paisley folk about their town is never easy. All of them have stories of their own, some passed on over generations and some based on local legend. Paisley Buddies know about their town and love to talk about it.

My thanks to all who helped me produce the book. Particular thanks go to the University of Paisley, the staff of Paisley Museum and Library for the use of archive material and to Chris and Nicola for their skill and patience in designing the book. I dedicate this book to Buddies present and future.

David Rowand   Paisley, Scotland 2001

Contents

King Robert III

Portrait of King Robert III who reigned from 1390-1406 "The worst of kings".

When Queen Victoria visited Paisley Abbey in 1888, she was reminded by Provost Cochran in his loyal address that, "Your Majesty's ancestor, Robert the Third, lies within its walls".Queen Victoria was moved to present the abbey with a magnificent marble tombstone, to mark the burial place of her ancestor, a king of Scots. The ravages of time had removed all traces of his grave, since his burial in 1406.

Monumental stone in white Sicilian marble in Paisley Abbey Choir, presented by Queen Victoria in 1888 to honour the burial place of her ancestor, Robert III, King of Scots.

Robert III's consort, Queen Annabella, "a lady good and pleasant and of excellent beauty", had once asked her husband why he had not made arrangements for a splendid tomb for himself. His reply was surprising.

"Bury me, I beg you, in a midden and write for my epitaph, Here lies the worst of kings and the most wretched of men in the whole kingdom."

Robert was born in 1337 the eldest son of King Robert II and christened John. He became Earl of Carrick, Baron Renfrew. When he ascended the throne of Scotland in 1390, he chose to reign under the title Robert III. The name John was thought to be unlucky for a Scots king and the nation still had bad memories of King John Balliol.

In 1381, as heir to the Scottish crown, he was appointed lieutenant of the kingdom by his father. The hope was that he would bring renewed justice to the country, particularly to the unruly Highlands where there existed a "savage, untamed race".

But all this went disastrously wrong. In 1388, Carrick was virtually incapacitated when he received a kick from a horse and, when he finally ascended the throne two years later at the age of 53, he was a physical and emotional cripple. He was described as "But a weak prince, unable to travel. Being bodily infirm, he had no grip on his kingdom". He was a depressive man, obsessed with his own disability.

To run the kingdom, he appointed his brother as Guardian of Scotland.

However, his injury did not prevent him fathering two bastard sons, two legitimate sons and four daughters! The king lost no time in honouring one of these 'natural' sons, Sir John Stewart, with the lands of Blackhall in Paisley.

In 1396, King Robert conferred Royal Burgh status on the town of Renfrew. In 1404, he secured all the old Stewart family lands in the Barony of Renfrew for his son and heir, James. At the same time he disjoined these lands from the Shire of Lanarkshire and created Renfrewshire. From that time to the present day, the eldest son of the monarch is known by right as Baron of Renfrew. The full title is "Baron Renfrew and Snawdon". Snawdon could well refer to the old lands of Sneddon in Paisley which adjoined and at sometime may have been part of the old Barony of Renfrew.

In 1398, the king gave a charter to Paisley Abbey, the church founded by his forbears. "We have taken under our protection the religious men of the monastery of Paisley, their lands and all their goods...... no one is to vex them".

During the reign of King Robert III, one chronicler lamented there was "no law in Scotland". The Highlands were still causing trouble. The king hit upon an idea to calm down the area. He invited the Clan Chattan and the Clan Kay, who were bitter enemies, to fight on a selected piece of ground at Perth. Thirty fully-armed men from each clan were to fight to the death. The king sat on a platform to oversee the contest. After a bloody battle in which only one of the Clan Chattan and ten of the Clan Kay were left alive, the king commanded the contest to end. For a long time after the Highlands remained peaceful. The king's idea had worked.

The king appointed his son and heir, David first Duke of Rothesay, to run the kingdom. To the king's sorrow, David was murdered in mysterious circumstances. This left James, the second son, as heir to the throne, but he was captured by the English and imprisoned in the Tower of London. King Robert heard of his son's capture while he was sitting down to supper at Rothesay Castle. The news of this further catastrophe was more than he could bear. "The news broke his heart... his spirit began to fade, his bodily strength eased away, he grew pale and such was his sorrow that he ate nothing more until he yielded his soul to his creator".

King Robert died at Rothesay on Palm Sunday, April 4th 1406. His corpse was conveyed to Paisley Abbey to be buried in a simple grave before the high altar, near to his grandmother Princess Marjory Bruce.

An ornately carved stone screen was built across the choir to honour the royal burial. The screen was emblazoned with coats of arms and effigies of abbey dignitaries. The sculpture was most probably carried out by masons from Glasgow Cathedral, where a similar screen still survives. Over the centuries, the abbey screen did not survive intact, but parts of it now form the the 'tomb' of Marjorie Bruce.

Paisley, although never made a Royal Burgh, can boast that royalty is always in our presence.

Palm-my-arm Ross

View of Castle built by Sir John Ross in 15th Century on the King's Inch, Renfrew.

Local legend tells of a David and Goliath contest that took place in the 15th Century between two champion wrestlers. The open-air match ended in the quick despatch and death of one of the combatants.

The venue was a field opposite the present day Glynhill Hotel on Renfrew Road. For centuries after, the field was known by locals as "Kempe Knowe",- the hill of the champion. The site consisted of a large mound of earth 60 feet in diameter, surrounded by a deep moat 15 feet wide. It remained until 1782, when it was ploughed up by a local farmer.

Tradition has it that the King of England had at his court a "Goliath" champion wrestler who had defeated all challengers. The king made a wager with the King of Scots and challenged him to find a wrestler who could match the English champion.

As a matter of national pride and after much searching, the King of Scots found a Scottish knight, Sir John Ross of Hawkhead, Paisley, who volunteered to meet the challenge. As a reward, should he be successful in defeating the English champion, Ross was to be given the lands and castle of "King's Inch" in Renfrew. This castle on an island on the Clyde was a favourite residence of the king.

Arrangements for the wrestling match were made. A mound of earth was constructed in the field and surrounded by a moat. When the eventful day arrived, a ring of fire was set on the mound and the moat filled with water. Only the victor could escape. The loser would be left to be burned or drowned.

The burial vault of "Palm-my-arm" Ross in Renfrew Parish Church.

The English champion, a gigantic man, stood within the circle. Beside him, Ross of Hawkhead, much smaller but more agile, stood dauntless. From neck to heel, Ross had covered himself in a tight-fitting animal skin with the flesh side worn outwards. This he had covered with oil, so that his appearance, although bizarre, was "smooth and glistening".

Amid shouts, the contest began. The Englishman pounced upon Ross and attempted to truss him up "as a hawk would a sparrow". The Englishman was thwarted when Ross, in his slippery costume, kept eluding his grasp. After many unsuccessful attempts to seize Ross, the frustrated English champion held out his own hands, inviting Ross to grasp them. Ross saw an opportunity to use his favourite wrestling hold. He seized the Englishman by the wrists and "with a sudden jerk, wrenched his opponent's shoulders out of their sockets and made easy work of him". The defeated champion was left to die. By his action, the victorious knight of Hawkhead, Sir John Ross, was given the nickname "Palm-my-arm Ross".

Although the King of Scots was delighted to win his wager against the King of England, he regretted his promise to give away his favourite castle on the King's Inch. He offered Ross an alternative of any other piece of land in the kingdom, but Ross was adamant and held the king to his promise. Ross said he would be glad to serve the king for that 'other' piece of land anytime in the future! Sir John Ross took possession of the "King's Inch" and there, on the ancient ruins of the High Steward's first castle, built a three-storey tower house known as the "Inch Castle".

Ross, the Paisley knight, "was sheathed in scaly armour so exquisitely polished that a fly could not walk upon it, for very smoothness".

Palm-my-arm Ross features again in Scottish history. Contemporary historians tell us that, in 1449, Sir John Ross of Hawkhead and other two Scottish knights fought with three foreign champions at Stirling, in presence of King James II and his court. On that occasion it was said that Ross was "sheathed in scaly armour, so exquisitely polished that a fly could not walk upon it for very smoothness". Further more, as he paced up and down the field of the tournament, "all eyes were so dazzled by his shining armour, that no one could look for any length of time upon him"! He had come a long way from his Paisley outfit! Such is the stuff of legend of what must have been a remarkable Paisley knight!

Palm-my-arm Ross died about 1474 and was buried in the chancel of the old pre- Reformation church at Renfrew. His monument can still be seen in the present-day Renfrew Parish Church The carved figures of this champion knight and his lady lie recumbent within a delicately carved, arched niche in the wall.

Abbot George Schaw

From a map of 1654, the Abbey appears surrounded by Abbot Schaw's great wall.

Seal of Abbot Schaw.

Paisley, as every good Buddie knows, is the largest burgh in Scotland. Soon, it may be granted city status and emerge from the shadows of "Big Brother Glasgow", as the truly independent town it always was.

The "City of Paisley" sounds good to the ear. A similar sound, sweet to the ear of the town's douce burghers, must have been heard in 1488, when Paisley became a fully-fledged burgh. This achievement, heralded in the mediaeval streets of Paisley, was due to the efforts of one remarkable man, George Schaw, Abbot of Paisley.

This learned ecclesiastic, much esteemed and highly respected, became abbot in 1472. His appointment was probably due to the fact that his aristocratic family, the Schaws of Sauchie and Greenock, had been influential at the court of the Scottish king. Schaw continued the family tradition and influence at court and became tutor to one of the sons of King James III.

During his term of office as abbot, Schaw played a large part in the development of the monastery, for he was both a builder and a capable administrator. He was continually adding to the abbey buildings. The larger part of the conventual buildings, now known as the Place of Paisley, though

Inscription stone from Abbot Schaw's great abbey wall, dated 1485.

much altered, we owe to him. The great gatehouse, built by Abbot Tervas, was surmounted by Schaw's steeple.

In the spring of 1485, Schaw built one of the wonders of mediaeval Scotland. This was a huge wall, one mile in circumference, which enclosed the abbey precincts. The great wall ran from the nave of the abbey along Abbey Close, Fisherow (Lawn Street) to the wallneuk (corner of Incle street) and continued southwards along Mill Street, until it ended on the bank of the River Cart. Inside, was a little park for deer and a newly laid-out garden and orchard. One visiting bishop described, with admiration, how magnificent were the carved statues set in niches and the inscriptions which adorned the handsomely-built wall. It was to last as a tourist attraction until the late 18th Century. One of the plaques from the wall is still preserved at Paisley Abbey.

Schaw was not only a 'true father' to his monks, but was the father of the Burgh of Paisley. In 1488, a considerable village had grown around the monastery. Its population, mainly artisans and tradesmen, formed a sizeable body of tenants under the protection of the monastery. They had to suffer heavy, sometimes unfair, taxes at the hands of the Royal Burgh of Renfrew. All this was put to rights by Abbot Schaw, who proposed that Paisley be made a burgh.

He first obtained sanction from the church, by telling them the income that could come from selling off feus of land in a new burgh. He then sought sanction from the state and used his friendship with young King James IV, to obtain a charter making the village of Paisley a burgh. The king willingly granted the privilege to "one to whom his family had been so much indebted". The charter of 1488 gave Paisley the right of buying and selling all sorts of goods within the burgh. It would have a market cross, that all important symbol of burgh dignity.

A small section of the old abbey wall can clearly be seen as part of the lower gable of this tenement nestling between the River Cart and Abbey Bridge. The tenement was demolished around the 1930s.

Paisley was no longer subject to Renfrew. Abbot Schaw lost no time in giving his new burgh the symbols of office. He appointed the first town council and presented the town with its tolbooth. The proud citizens of Paisley erected their market cross, doubtless encouraged by Abbot Schaw. Soon after, in a night raid, the men of the Royal Burgh of Renfrew came to the new burgh, eager to destroy this new rival in trade. They 'danged doon' the market cross, of which Paisley was so proud.

The indignant Abbot Schaw spoke to the king on his next visit to the abbey, complaining of the way his Paisley burgesses had been treated by their neighbours. Renfrew was forced to proclaim the king's displeasure at their market cross and to punish the men who "had destroyed the hewn work of the new market town". Not to be outdone, Paisley men raided Renfrew, to destroy its market cross.

Renfrew took legal action. The learned Abbot Schaw, always protective of his new burgh, rose to the challenge. He threatened to sue Renfrew for reparation of back-dated dues. Schaw argued that, since Paisley had been given its Charter of Regality in 1451, it should not have been paying dues to Renfrew for the last 37 years. At this threat to their coffers, Royal Renfrew backed down.

Abbot Schaw confirmed the royal charter of 1488 to the burgh in 1490. The following year, under direction from the Pope, Schaw absolved the young, remorseful King James IV before the high altar at Paisley Abbey. He made penance for any guilt he may have had in the death of his father King James III, at the Battle of Sauchieburn.

In 1495, Abbot Schaw was appointed lord High Treasurer of Scotland. He served for two years. In later life, the abbot built a manor house at nearby Blackston, as a summer retreat from the daily pressures of his office. After a long and busy life, Abbot Schaw spent more and more time at Blackston Manor. When monastery business at Paisley required his authority or sanction while he was staying at Blackston, the saying "you'll have to get a line from Blackston" became common. This saying is still in occasional use in Paisley today! After serving 25 years as Abbot of Paisley, he retired in 1498 and died in 1505.

Bridge of Paisley

The view drawn in 1693 shows the town's only bridge. First mentioned in 1490 and rebuilt at the close of the 16th century. It connected the Abbey to Paisley Cross. Clearly shown is the old custom booth and port at one side of the bridge.

A bridge in Paisley spanning the River Cart is mentioned as far back as 1490. When a bridge was first built near Paisley Cross is unknown, but we do know that it was built to connect the abbey with its satellite village of Paisley on the other side of the river.

This old structure was known for centuries as the Bridge of Paisley and stood until about 1586, when it was rebuilt. In those days, the only way to come into town from the east was via Paisley's one and only bridge. By the end of the 16th Century, the old bridge had fallen into a ruinous state and the town council did not have sufficient funds to make the necessary repairs. The council appealed to King James VI for some help. In 1598, the king granted a royal charter which enabled Paisley Town Council to levy custom or toll on the owners of every horse, cow or sheep passing over the bridge. To prevent unwarranted passage over the bridge, a custom booth or town's port was erected at the town end of the bridge. Those failing to pay the toll would have their goods or cattle poinded. Over a period of nineteen years, the monies raised were used to maintain and repair the bridge.

Paisley's only bridge was important for another reason. During the scourge of the pestilence or plague, such as the visitation of 1603, the bridge would be roped off and watched by guards appointed by the town council. For its time, this precaution showed great sense, but, alas, no precautions could ward off this disease and many times the town suffered.

This bridge was built in 1783 to designs by architect James Brown. In 1828, it was widened and continually repaired until it was finally replaced in 1882.

In January 1614, Paisley Town Council had collected enough custom dues to appoint "six of the best skilled persons to point the stonework of the bridge at the proper season of the year". In 1635, the council passed an act to close the Bridge Port on Sundays, with the exception of the wicket gate which allowed pedestrians to cross. This was to prevent carriers crossing the bridge and breaking the Sabbath!

In 1677, custom duties were further imposed on the bridge. People bringing in butter, cheese, meat, horses, cows, sheep, cattle, fodder and timber had to pay quite heavy tolls to the burgh. However, there were some exceptions granted. Any man returning from market via the bridge with an unsold horse did not have to pay a penny!

In 1702, Paisley's old bridge suffered a major disaster when one of its two arches collapsed in to the River Cart below. This was a major blow to the town's economy, as traffic came almost to a standstill. Traders had to use the two fords in the river, one just below the Hammills and the other at Sneddon to get to town. This state of affairs lasted a year, until funds became available for the bridge's repair.

The long-standing custom booth on the bridge was abandoned in 1763. It was duly removed by the council, as they considered it "useless and no longer needed". Besides, it obstructed the view from Smithhills to the main part of the town.

St. James Bridge was newly built in 1882 in keeping with the style of the new Town Hall. This view, looking towards Paisley Cross, dates from the late 1930s.

Twenty years later, it was found that the old bridge had become unsafe and had to be demolished. The council built a new bridge which was much wider than the old to cope with the increase in traffic. The two-arched stone bridge was designed by Kilbarchan architect James Brown. Its maximum width was 29 feet and each arch spanned 46 feet. In 1827, this bridge, too, fell into disrepair. When funds became available, the council instructed James Donaldson to carry out the repairs to the masonry work, while the repointing of the stonework was entrusted to the slater James Gillespie. In 1828, this bridge was widened to keep pace with street development. James Brown's original design for the bridge was well conceived. It had been built of good durable stone on strong foundations and had with stood many years of seasonal floods. Yet, its days were numbered.

With the building of the nearby Town Hall in 1881, it was decided to remove the old bridge and replace it with a splendid new structure more in keeping with the style of the Town Hall. The fine new bridge was completed in 1882 and, after much debate at council level, was named St James Bridge. This elegant, two-arched, stone structure with its balustraded parapets was designed by William Lynn, the architect of the Town Hall. At last, Paisley had a bridge of which she could be proud. In 1929, this bridge was also widened, again to cope with ever-increasing traffic. Unfortunately, the elegant, Victorian, stone balustrades on the north side were removed with the building of the Piazza between the years 1968-70.

It appears that bridge building in Paisley over the centuries was fraught with difficulties, both financial and physical. Today, the St James Bridge remains one of the main thoroughfares of the town, but, thankfully, passers-by are not asked to pay for the privilege like the Buddies of old!

Mr Andrew Knox

A view of Knox's house jutting into High Street, about 1900. The building, erected in 1594, was reputed to be the oldest inhabited house in Paisley. It was finally demolished in the early decades of this century. (photo courtesy Paisley Museum)

The famous reformer John Knox described Paisley as a "Nest of Papistrie". The town was one of the last places in Scotland to turn to the new Protestant religion. The accusation was directed not so much against the town, but against one of its former abbots, John Hamilton. Hamilton, who stood as champion for the old Catholic religion, was an old rival of Knox.

Hamilton, who also held the office of Archbishop of St Andrews, Primate of Scotland and who recently had ruled church and state, made a rather affronting and, at the same time, very humbling mission back to Paisley, where he had served as last abbot of the monastery. Standing on top of a dunghill in one of Paisley's narrow streets, Archbishop Hamilton, Primate of Scotland, beseeched a small crowd of onlookers to return to the faith of the mother church. He blessed the religious waverers in the street and praised those who had remained in the old faith. Hamilton was charged with the crime of "attempting to restore Popery in the town of Paisley".

A carved oak panel taken from the mantelpiece of Andrew Knox's house. The monogram M.A.E.K. stands for Master Andrew and Elizabeth Knox, his spouse. This carved panel can be seen in Paisley Museum.

Such were the scenes in Paisley at the time of the Reformation. The first Protestant minister to arrive in the town was 'locked out' of the abbey and some early ministers were even stoned by the people of Paisley! Succeeding ministers could not find accommodation in the town. Some ministers accused the citizens of Paisley of having 'manifest vices' and suffering from a 'contempt of discipline'.

The time came, however, when to profess being a Roman Catholic or even to hold secret services became a dangerous game. In 1585, to deal with the Catholics in Paisley, a Protestant 'hit man', Andrew Knox, was appointed as minister of Paisley Abbey. Like his more famous relative, John Knox the reformer, Andrew Knox, too, was a zealous fanatic in the fight against Catholicism. His success in uncovering secret Catholics had commended him to the king and privy council. One of his first actions in his new charge at Paisley was to complain to the General Assembly that the former Abbot of Paisley, John Hamilton, was a "receiver of Jesuits".

By 1592, Knox had achieved national fame for his activities. So successful was he in detecting Catholics, that he was given the king's commission "to seek out and apprehend all Papists, Jesuits, priests and suspect traffickers with the King of Spain and other foreigners which would subvert God's true religion".

At that time throughout the land, the fear was that Philip, King of Spain, would land a second Armada and re-establish Catholicism. Conspirators were everywhere. George Ker, who was thought to be one, was seen in the neighbourhood of Paisley. Knox managed to track Ker down to Fairlie, just as he was about to sail on his treacherous Spanish mission. After a thorough search, Knox found incriminating documents hidden in the sleeve of a sailor on Ker's ship. Ker was arrested and jailed. In 1592, for this notable capture, Knox received the high praise of the Privy Council.

Five years later, Knox got wind of a plot that Ailsa Craig would be seized and filled with Spanish troops. To pre-empt a landing by the Spaniards, Knox and his 'armed' friends occupied the island. The Spaniards arrived, led by a local conspirator, Hugh Barclay of Ladyland. Barclay had previously been imprisoned for his religion, but had made his escape to Spain, where he "trafficked and had intelligence with the enemy of true religion".

Knox demanded Barclay's surrender. Barclay drew his sword, but being hard pressed in the ensuing fight, stepped backwards, fell into the sea and was drowned. Knox was blamed for his death and now became the subject of a death threat by Barclay's friends. Knox, now a worried man, appealed to the king for protection. The king praised him for his "loyal and good service" and forbade anyone to molest him.

Andrew Knox was disliked in Paisley. He was too fanatical, zealous and overbearing. His impulsive nature led him into difficulties with his congregation and even his neighbour. In 1594, he built a three-storey, crow-stepped gabled house in Paisley's High Street. He thoughtlessly put windows into one of the gables which overlooked his neighbour's property. His neighbour, John Maxwell of Stanely, rightly argued against this invasion of privacy and took his complaint to the burgh court. Maxwell won his case and Knox was ordered to built up the offending window. Even the rainwater spout from the rear of Knox's house was designed to 'rin doon' and discharge on to Maxwell's back yard! Knox indeed was a nasty neighbour.

To get his revenge for losing the court case, Knox reported to the church authority that Maxwell had not attended communion for some time. This was a serious accusation at that time. Maxwell explained to the church authority that he had not attended church because of the 'deadly feud' between the two parties and that he had simply switched worship to the parish church in Renfrew.

In 1604, Knox, now known in Paisley as the 'Papist catcher', was suspended temporarily from his ministry for striking a Paisley burgess called Stewart, "so violently upon the head with a key, to the effusion of his blood".

Paisley was glad to rid itself of such a violent man of the cloth. The people were relieved when, in 1605, he was appointed Bishop of the Isles by King James VI. Knox never returned to Paisley Abbey to discharge his final duties as their minister, but deserted his congregation at Paisley for ever.

Captain William Cochrane

View of the Place of Paisley the principal residence of the Dundonalds since 1653, where William, 7th Earl of Dundonald was born in 1729.

The Cochrane family had been well established in Renfrewshire since the 12th Century. In 1653, the family purchased the Lordship of Paisley and made their principal residence in the Place of Paisley. Throughout the centuries, the family were known as the 'Fighting Cochranes'. Some even served as bodyguards to the King of France in the famous 'Garde Ecossaise'.

Master William Cochrane, who was born in 1729 at the Place of Paisley, was destined to follow in the family's military tradition. When he was only eight, his father, the 6th Earl of Dundonald, died and young William, the future 7th Earl, was put under the care of guardians. One of these was his older cousin, William Cochrane of Ferguslie, who, in 1745, openly supported the Jacobite cause of 'Bonnie Prince Charlie'. Cochrane of Ferguslie had joined the ranks of the victorious Jacobite army at the battle of Prestonpans.

William was inspired by his cousin's adventures and, when he was sixteen, he decided to leave Paisley and join the Jacobite army. He was still a minor and his guardians kept an eye on the restless boy. One Sunday morning, he managed to elude his guardians and stole away to Glasgow in the company of a manservant.

The coat-of-arms of the ancient and illustrious Cochrane family, whose direct line of descent ended with the death of Captain William Cochrane.

The pair hired horses and set out for Edinburgh. At this time the capital was under the spell of the 'Bonnie Prince', whose presence and appearance had captivated all in the city. By nightfall, William and his manservant had reached the outskirts of Edinburgh. As they approached the city, they met up with a coach full of women and children. They accompanied the coach to the West Port, where they found the city gates closed and guarded by Jacobite Highland soldiers. William, his manservant and the occupants of the coach found great difficulty in getting past the guards. The Highland soldiers spoke in Gaelic, so neither side could make themselves understood. The loud, exasperated shouts of the parties were overheard by the garrison in Edinburgh Castle, high above the West Port. The castle was still in the hands of Hanoverian troops and, soon, their cannon, loaded with grape-shot, was pointed downwards and fired into the darkness of the West Port.

The following day, the Caledonian Mercury newspaper reported that a coach full of women and children had been fired upon. One woman had been shot through the hip.....and a horse and servant had been killed. It was William Cochrane's horse who had been shot from under him and his manservant who had been killed. William's narrow escape from death did not alter his determination to join the rebel army. He remained in the city for two days, but his Edinburgh relatives after much persuasion, convinced him to return to Paisley. Unlike his cousin, William never joined Prince Charlie's army.

Portrait of the young William Cochrane, 7th Earl of Dundonald, who gallantly, but fatally, led his men at the Battle of Louisburg against the French.

At the of 21, William Cochrane became the 7th Earl of Dundonald. However, domestic life in Paisley was too mundane for such an adventurous young man. He sold off some of his lands at Laighpark in Paisley and went to Holland to join the Scots Brigade. He served as captain for a few years and then returned to Paisley where he took an active part making 'improvements' to the town. What his 'improvements' were, we shall see.

As soldiering was in his blood, the once idealistic young Jacobite changed loyalties and entered the service of the Hanoverian King George II, as Captain in the 17th Regiment of Foot. In 1757, to raise money before leaving for America with his regiment, William gave instructions to sell off some more of his lands in Paisley. These were the old Abbey Gardens "very advantageously situated upon the River Cart". These lands contained the mediaeval abbey gatehouse, built by Abbot Tervas and part of Abbot Schaw's much admired enclosing wall. Prospective purchasers were informed that excellent material from the old buildings could be had from this site and a vast quantity of hewn stones would be available. So began the asset stripping of part of Paisley's mediaeval abbey.

In the struggle to rid Canada of the French, William's regiment was dispatched to lay siege to Fort Louisburg, a French stronghold on the island of Cape Breton. The siege began in 1758. Captain William Cochrane, 7th Earl of Dundonald, was commanding a Company of Grenadiers entrenched in a forward position when the position was suddenly attacked by several hundred French troops. William and his company fought gallantly, but, before reinforcements could be brought up, William was fatally wounded.

In his dispatches, General Wolfe made a remark on the Earl's death. "You will have heard the story of my Lord Dundonald's surprise defeat and death...." When the Earl was killed he was only 29 years old. He had never married and so ended the original line of descent of the Cochrane family, which had lasted over 500 years.

The Grammar School at Churchill

The third Grammar School, a neat little building, proudly displaying the old foundation stone above the architraved doorway. Built 1802. Restored 1999.

Another part of Paisley's architectural heritage was recently restored stone by stone. The restoration is all the more pleasant as the building is listed and stands within the Oakshaw Conservation Area. The building, now restored for future generations, was the old Grammar School of Paisley. This modest building, nestles between the former High and Middle Churches at the top of Churchill.

The restoration of this building is significant in the history of Paisley, as it was the third in line of Grammar Schools to be built in Paisley. The school was first completed and opened to scholars in 1802. There is a tradition that, when the scholars abandoned their former school, built in School Wynd in 1753, they marched in a formal procession with flags flying and drums beating to their splendid new school. The old school in School Wynd had outgrown its usefulness. It had been an overcrowded, cramped, 'but and ben' affair, where, due to the "unhealthy state of the school several boys had been removed due to their indisposition".

23

John Peddie,
Rector of the Grammar School, 1797-1833.

The new school promised better things. No expense was spared by the town council in its erection. "It was a most substantial commodious building". It boasted a large single classroom, 49ft x 32ft, on the ground floor and living quarters for the rector above! The elegant little two-storey, stone-built building was designed by a local architect, Robert Barr, whose handsome fee amounted to five guineas. The only defect it had was the "scantiness of the playground".

The fact that a new Grammar School was built at all was largely through the efforts of one man, John Peddie, the school's rector. He was looked upon in Paisley as a man of quality and highly regarded. It was he who had made a stand to have the new school built on a site at Churchill. Since 1797, when he had been appointed the rector he had agitated against the town council for a new school building. But, over the years, the penurious council had the habit of putting this important matter off their agenda.

John Peddie finally threatened to resign unless a better building was provided for his scholars. As he was a good rector and highly prized by the council, they finally agreed to his demands and provided a new school at a cost of over a thousand pounds. The council's money was well spent as, in the new building, the school's academic achievements reached a golden age. The cultivation of classical literature, logic, Latin and Greek established the school's fine reputation in the world of academia.

The hard-working headmaster, who trained his pupils to such high standards, felt underpaid by the council. In 1808, he once more threatened to resign, to go and teach in the Grammar School of Glasgow, but again he won the day. To pay for his increased salary, the school fees were raised by half a guinea per pupil!

When the new grammar school was built in 1802, the town council forgot to remove the ancient stone tablet from the old school in School Wynd. This was considered a matter of concern by some 'old boys' of the school. The old foundation stone bore the words "The Gramar Scuil 1586" and had adorned the wall of the very first school in School Wynd. Although the school received its royal charter in 1576, it had taken the council the space of ten years to actually build the first school! Perhaps the council of these days 'could have done better' by taking note of the school motto "Learn boy or get out"! The

When the new school was completed in 1802, the council forgot to remove this ancient school tablet from School Wynd to its new abode at Churchill. After a delay of 11 years, it was finally set in position!

old stone was eventually removed and proudly set into its new position above the entrance door of the new school at Churchill, but only after a delay of eleven years!

One strange, ancient custom was carried forward to the new school. At Candlemas, in February, all the scholars were assembled together in school. When their names were called out, each pupil in turn would walk up to the rector and give him a sum of money. This could vary from half-a-crown to a guinea. On receipt of the money, the rector would give each pupil an orange from a large basket he carried at his side. The boy who gave most money was declared 'King for the Day', amid shouts from the pupils. This rather degrading custom could give the rector and his staff an extra income of as much as £40!

Peddie retired in 1833. Under his successor, William Brunton, the school curriculum was greatly extended to include all branches of mathematics and commercial education. Incidentally, part of his contract as rector was to pay for any broken windows in the school a very common occurrence with schoolboys of those days!

Despite being extended, once again the school building in Churchill became too small. It was replaced by a new, larger building nearby which boasted five classrooms. This, the fourth school building, was opened in 1863 and called the "Grammar School and Academy".

Over the years, the old building at Churchill, Paisley's third Grammar School, was abandoned. Its windows were boarded up and the structure left to the elements. Today, it is has been beautifully restored.

Thomas Bissland, father and son

Medallion portrait of Thomas Bissland timber merchant (1722-1804), by John Henning. (courtesy Paisley Museum).

It was in 1756 that James Tannahill, the father of Robert the poet, came from Kilmarnock to work as a weaver in Paisley. That same year, Thomas Bissland and his brother came from Drymen to Paisley to ply their trade as wrights. Their sons were destined to become great friends.

Thomas Bissland became a very successful business man in his adopted town, trading as a timber merchant in the Baltic trade. In 1760, he formed a partnership with Charles Maxwell of Merksworth, a local old-monied laird. At this time, Paisley was rapidly expanding. House after house was being built and street after street was being laid out, particularly in the west part of Paisley at Broomlands and in the east around the old Abbey Gardens.

Maxwell and Bissland carried an extensive business in trading timber to and from the Baltic and the Mediterranean, all in their own private fleet of ships. Due to the large number of houses being built in Paisley, the demand for their timber made the partners very prosperous.

Over the years since his arrival in Paisley, Thomas Bissland had moved from being a humble joiner or wright up to the high social circles of Paisley. In 1771, the same year in which he was appointed Burgh Treasurer, he married Margaret Kibble. Her father owned the large estate of Auchentorlie at Seedhill Road. In 1785, Bissland acquired some thirty acres of this estate from his father-in-law and built a large mansion called Auchentorlie House. This house must have turned a few heads, as it was built in the fashionable style of the day to look like a Gothic castle.

In addition to this gentleman's country seat, Bissland also owned several houses in Paisley. One of these was a large town house in St Mirren's Wynd called the 'Blakhole'.

In 1765, he rebuilt this old house five storeys high to house six families. The house was so tall that the top most families felt that they could almost touch the sky! No town planning in those days.

People in Paisley were still building many new houses forty years later, making Bissland a wealthy man. As a man of standing he could well afford to have his likeness taken for posterity in the newly fashionable medium of a portrait medallion. In 1801, at the venerable age of 79, Bissland sat for his

In 1798, Thomas Bissland, the son, bought a large country house with a castle-like frontage at Ferguslie. In 1806 Bissland bought the whole estate of Ferguslie, for the enormous sum of £10,000.

portrait. Like Bissland, the remarkable young artist who sat down to take his likeness, had been a wright in Paisley, but had abandoned the hatchet and saw to pursue his talent as a modeller. The artist's name was John Henning. Henning was to achieve fame as a leading portrait medallionist in later years. Three years after his portrait was completed, Thomas Bissland died and was buried in Paisley Abbey Yard.

His only son, who was also called Thomas, had been born in Paisley in 1772 and, on coming of age, had begun business in Paisley as a cotton spinner. Like his father, he was successful and became wealthy. In 1798, he bought a large country house at Ferguslie with a castle-like frontage which had a similar style to his father's house at Auchentorlie. The previous owner of this house was a prosperous inn keeper called John Gibb. Gibb had owned a hay-weighing machine in King Street, where the Hay Weighs public house now stands.

In 1806, Bissland purchased the whole estate of Ferguslie, about 156 acres, from the Paisley Burgh for the enormous sum of £10,000. A frequent visitor to this beautiful country estate was the poet Robert Tannahill. His poems enshrined "Sweet Ferguslie as a "dear sacred grove" and it was "Here that nature first waked me to rapture and love." During the course of his frequent visits to Ferguslie and its wood,Tannahill became a close friend of Thomas Bissland. He knew him as "Tom o the Wood". Tannahill said of him "A

The huge mansion house at Ferguslie became the home of Thomas Coats.
The procession seen passing the house in 1868 was making its way to the official
opening of the Fountain Gardens, donated to the town by Coats.

gentleman whom indigence never solicited in vain". Strangely, Tannahill penned an epitaph to Bissland in 1806, saying in his first line, "Ever green be the sod o'er kind Tom o the Wood", even although Bissland was still very much alive. Tannahill thought so much of his friend that he hoped these words would be inscribed on Bissland's tomb after his death.

However, Thomas Bissland outlived Tannahill, who committed suicide in 1810. The year after Tannahill's death, Bissland's business failed due to the general distress in commerce suffered in Paisley and elsewhere. Shortly after this, Bissland received the appointment of Collector of Customs at Greenock. He worked until retiring in 1836. Bissland then left Greenock to stay with his son in England. He died there in 1846, aged 72.

The huge mansion house at Ferguslie became the home of Thomas Coats the thread magnate who could look out of his windows and keep a watchful eye on his huge thread mills across the road.

Gaels and umbrellas.

The old church is pavilion roofed and rubble built. Its simplicity reflects the austere nature of meeting-house religion. The porch on the left, which was added in 1909, is the work of the Paisley architect T.G. Abercrombie.

Large numbers of Highlanders arrived in Paisley between the years 1770 and 1780. Highland clearances and hunger drove them from their traditional homes in Argyll and the Isles to large towns like Paisley.

When they arrived in Paisley, some almost destitute, many Highland men took work as labourers or farmhands. The women usually entered domestic service or worked in the local bleachfields and dyeworks.

To accommodate the ever increasing number of Highland worshippers, a Gaelic Chapel was erected in Oakshaw in 1793. To those who did not speak or wholly understand the English language the new church was a blessing, as the sermons were initially given in Gaelic. The idea of building such a chapel for these poor, forlorn and sometimes homesick Gaels was thanks to one man in particular, Alexander Weir.

He, too, had come from the Highlands some time before. He had been born near Inverary in 1742. When his father married for a second time, young Alexander came to the Lowlands at the age of eight. In the course of time, Alexander came to live and work in Paisley and set himself up in business as a cloth merchant at Paisley Cross.

The oval plaque in English and Latin fronting the old church was designed to welcome the original Gaelic-speaking congregation!

By all accounts, Alexander Weir was regarded as a very talented figure of high intelligence, who took a deep interest in the social, religious and political life of Paisley. Such was his social standing in the town, that in 1779, he stood as witness for the young Alexander Wilson (later to become Paisley's world-famous ornithologist) when he signed apprenticeship papers indenturing him to the weaving trade. On another occasion, Alexander Weir, as one of the rich merchants of Paisley, was one of the more important persons invited to dine with the poet Robert Burns on his visit to the town.

In 1793, Weir purchased a large piece of ground at Caversbank, Oakshaw. Two years later, he generously transferred ownership to the trustees of the newly-formed Gaelic Chapel. At the same time, he drew up the constitution of the new church. A branch of the Church of Scotland, the Oakshaw building was one of three such Gaelic churches to be built in the Clyde Valley. The church was to serve Gaelic speakers only, but the inscribed plaque erected outside the church proclaimed the "Gaelic Chapel" in English! To further confuse the Highlanders, the date of the church's foundation is in Latin numerals. This could only happen in Paisley!

Perhaps this liberal attitude to spelling reflected Weir's politics. He was a staunch Liberal. Despite this, he was elected to the Tory Town Council in 1781, out of respect for his support for the social and moral comfort of the people of Paisley.

In 1793, Alexander Weir was elected president of "The Society for the Reformation of Manners". This influential and powerful Paisley institution was founded by local gentlemen to keep its watchful eye on the morals and

Weir brought to Paisley the first umbrella ever seen. The year was 1788. The picture shows a lady of fashion sporting an umbrella near Paisley Cross in 1835.

religious habits of the 'criminal classes' of the town. The members of the society considered it their duty to report on any such activities to the town authorities, who would, in turn, severely punish the culprits. Keeping an "unclean house' and, of course, not attending the kirk on a Sunday were considered to be serious offenses!

Weir's role in the history of Paisley is twofold. He was the founding father of the Gaelic Chapel, but his other claim to fame is perhaps more mundane. As a ruling elder in the High Church of Paisley, he was called upon to attend the General Assembly of 1788. When he was in Edinburgh, he purchased an item in the latest fashion, an umbrella. He brought it back to Paisley and caused a sensation. The people of Paisley had never seen such a new-fangled apparatus. This strangely-shaped object had a covering of oil cloth designed to keep out the rain. Soon, Paisley had its own umbrella manufacturer and fashionable ladies and gentlemen paraded them through the town.

After Weir's death in 1819, the famous umbrella was handed down in the family. In 1872, Weir's grandson, John Lorimer, had it re-covered in a cotton fabric. At that time, it was unquestionably the oldest umbrella in Paisley.

Many thousands of umbrellas have been used and worn out in the burgh since the very first one appeared and umbrella manufacturers have come and gone in Paisley, just like the Gaelic Chapel. The old building, once the home of the Highland faithful, has been converted into residential flats. Alexander Weir would be pleased to know that the Gaelic Chapel he founded way back in 1793, now lies protected under an umbrella of a different sort, "The Oakshaw Conservation Area"!

Mrs Isabella Graham

Portrait of Isabella Graham.

Isabella Marshall was born in Lanarkshire in July 1742, to deeply Christian parents. With a £100 legacy from her grandfather, Isabella, unusually for a girl in those days, was sent to a private boarding school. There, she excelled in the study of moral and religious knowledge.

From Hamilton, the family moved to Elderslie and rented the old estate once owned by the illustrious Wallace family. Isabella, who was a pious child, took delight in the old estate, where she had a secret place to pray to God. As she grew older, she worshiped with her family at the Laigh Kirk in New Street, Paisley, where she was influenced by its celebrated minister, Rev. John Witherspoon.

In 1789, Isabella opened a school in New York, where George Washington honoured her with his patronage.

In 1765, Isabella married Dr John Graham, who was a practising physician and a gentleman of liberal education and high social standing in Paisley. A year after their marriage, Dr Graham, was commissioned as a field surgeon and ordered to join his regiment, the Royal Americans, stationed in Canada. Isabella joined her husband in Montreal. During the regiments time in Canada, Isabella bore three daughters. Up to this time, her husband had seen no military action and Isabella found the social life of the regiment agreeable, but, soon, the Grahams found themselves caught up in the American War of Independence.

They were ordered to make their way to the British garrison on the island of Antigua. Isabella settled in Antigua with her young family and two young Indian girl servants. When her husband returned from the Caribbean, where he had been helping to quell a local rebellion, he found his wife, Isabella, inconsolable. She had just received news of her mother's death in Scotland. Dr Graham roused her from her grief by saying, "God might call you to a severer trial by taking my life". Sadly, the words proved prophetic, as, shortly after, in November 1774, he was to die of fever.

Isabella, now a widow with three children and expecting another, found herself in dire straits in a foreign land. She had less than £200 remaining of her husband's estate. Her friends urged her to sell the two Indian girls, her late husband's property, but Isabella adamantly refused to do this, saying that, "I can not not make merchandise of my fellow creatures". One of the girls remained behind in Antigua, the other travelled with Isabella to Paisley.

After a long voyage across the Atlantic, Isabella and her family landed in Belfast, then boarded a ship for Scotland. The ship encountered a great storm which lasted nine hours and the rudder and masts were carried away. Eventually, the ship struck a rock on the coast near Ayr and ended on a sandbank, where the passengers were eventually rescued. During the panic of the storm, only Isabella had remained "composed and ready to meet her maker."

She came to Paisley, where she opened a small school. The slender income from this and a widow's pension of £16 a year were the family's only means of support. "Her breakfast and supper were porridge, her dinner, potatoes and salt, her children were dressed in home spun clothes. She wished to owe no person anything, but love."

To make extra money, Isabella made muslin dresses and had them shipped to the West Indies, but her bad luck continued. The venture was a financial disaster when her precious cargo was captured by an enemy French frigate.

Various friends consoled her and suggested that a woman of her education should open a boarding school in Edinburgh. Just as she was selling all her furniture for the move to Edinburgh, she received a letter. It contained money from her shipping agent. Unknown to Isabella, her agent had insured her valuable cargo for loss. Her luck had turned!

Her school in Edinburgh, opened in 1780, was a total success and daughters of the Edinburgh aristocracy flocked to her school. Her former minister Dr Witherspoon, now a famous man in America, paid her a visit. He persuaded her to go to America, where there were better opportunities for teaching wealthy young ladies.

In July, 1789, Isabella arrived in New York. She built up her new school from five pupils to fifty, within a month of opening. Even General George Washington honoured her with his patronage! Isabella was now earning good money, but she never forgot the poor and laid aside a tenth of her income for charity.

Throughout the remainder of her life in America, she visited the poor, gave them bread and work, provided hostels for orphaned children, founded a Widow's Society and fought against slavery and gambling. In 1811, she founded the New York Magdalen Society for 'fallen women'.

During the last two years of her life, despite ill health, Isabella still visited the distressed families, prisons and hospitals of New York.In 1814, she set up the Sabbath Adult School in Greenwich Village, to improve the meagre education of young men and women. On 17th July that year she died, worn out by a selfless life helping others less fortunate than herself. New York City looked on her death as a great public loss. All the churches of the city praised her life's work and all the charities with which she had been associated paid tribute to this remarkable Scots lady.

William and John Hart, town jailors

The old tolbooth where William Hart was appointed the town's first official jailor.

William Hart, who was a weaver in Townhead, was appointed one of the town officers for Paisley in 1774. At this time and, for twenty years afterwards, all the town officers also acted as the town jailors.

Then, the town council decided it would be better to appoint a full-time jailor, who could devote his whole time to looking after the prisoners in Paisley Tolbooth. In 1801, William Hart was recommended as the first town jailor. He took two days to consider the offer, as the post only carried an annual salary of £20. In addition, he was to find three guarantors and the sum of £500 as surety. He did finally accept the offer when he realised there were perks to the job. The jailor would be allowed to accept the jail dues from his prisoners and, more importantly, would be allowed to sell porter and ale to the prisoners and their visitors!

The dues payable by the prisoners to the jailor had been fixed by the council. The cost of their board and lodgings was included and the astute William Hart realised he was on to a good thing. He had a guaranteed income from such a "secure and safe place", from which his 'clients' could not escape! If you were a burgess of Paisley, an overnight stay in prison brought Hart, twopence, while a non-burgess had to pay double that amount.

The old County Bridewell or Jail, where John Hart served as the first governor in 1820.

Hart's duties included keeping the prison clean, cleaning the stairs, sweeping the rooms and passages, removing and carrying away all "filth and nastiness". Supervising this kept him busy, but his most important task was to visit each room morning and evening, to ensure that no windows, walls or floors had been breached. The keys to the whole prison were to be kept in Hart's own possession and not to be entrusted to any of the servants. Despite Hart's precautions, some enterprising prisoners managed to escape and were never found!

Many a Paisley Buddie was incarcerated for debt of even the smallest sums. In those days debtors had special privileges while in prison. Their friends and relatives were allowed to visit them and console them with porter and ale. These were sold to them by the jailor. William Hart did a roaring trade in the "howff". This was a room under the tolbooth steeple set aside for drinking. Hart was a kindly man, who sometimes allowed the inmates credit for their board, lodging and drink and, in certain circumstances, even lent them money.

Although Hart was only the humble town jailor, he was looked upon by the citizens of Paisley as a very humane and highly-respected man. When he was admitted as a member of the Tailor's Society in 1799, Hart considered this a great honour. He died in 1812, after serving the community for the long period of 38 years.

John Hart, the town jailor, accompanied by his two faithful greyhounds, talking to a man on horseback in Causeyside Street.

He was succeeded in office by his eldest son John. John had been his father's assistant since 1808 and, like his father, was a kind-hearted, genial man and much respected in the community. The annual salary had increased to £40, but it was still not even sufficient to pay an assistant. To supplement his income, he, like his father, sold drink to the inmates. One of the first items on his agenda was to erect a large painted signboard "Ale and Porter Sold Here" above the prison door!

John Hart, needless to say, was greatly liked by those under his charge, whether debtors or criminals. He sold as "much malt liquor as they deserved"! Once again, the howff, a large, commodious room on the ground floor of the tolbooth was "fu and happy". Hart sold such a large quantity of drink that nearby publicans were green with envy. They grudgingly saw John Hart accumulating wealth. Under Hart's regime, the prisoners had "a jolly time of it". They comforted and consoled themselves in the howff, despite their loss of liberty.

While John Hart was a conscientious jailor, he did not spend more time in prison than duty required. He was a keen sportsman and fond of hare-coursing. He kept a brace of greyhounds and often joined local lairds at friendly meetings. Hart was considered to keep the best-trained greyhounds in the West of Scotland. His portly figure, dressed in knee breeches with white 'rig and fur' stockings, made him a familiar sight in the streets of Paisley, where he was always accompanied by his two faithful greyhounds.

In 1820, John Hart was appointed as the first governor of the new County Jail in County Square. He stayed in the governor's house inside the jail.

The prisoners, the subjects of his care, were transferred from the old tolbooth to the new prison. The magistrates declared "that such a transfer shall not be deemed or taken to be an escape". In 1825, some prisoners did escape, but got only as far as nearby County Square, where they stumbled across the 79th Regiment on church parade! Much to the relief of Hart, the prisoners all dejectedly returned to their cells, neatly closing their doors behind them!

John Hart's successor as governor was the appropriately named Mr Bird. Only in Paisley did we have a real live jail-bird! The jail, built like a mediaeval stronghold, dominated the centre of the town until the 1960s. It had some famous visitors. The prison reformer, Elizabeth Fry, inspected its conditions and, in later times, the great Harry Houdini when touring in Paisley with his act, made an escape from Paisley Jail as part of a publicity stunt. Imagine anyone wanting to escape from Paisley !

The Renfrewshire Tontine

View of the Renfrewshire Tontine C.1860. Gauze Street on left of building.
Silk Street (later named Bank Street) to right. First built 1780-2.
Demolished around 1969 to make way for the complex of administrative buildings of
Renfrew District Council in Cotton St. (photo courtesy of Paisley Museum)

In the late 18th Century, Paisley was a hive of industry, with the click-clack of shuttles at every street corner. The production of silks, lawns, muslins, gauzes and thread, all of the finest quality, kept the town fully occupied. Many new workers, eager for employment, arrived in Paisley, which was fast becoming one of the principal towns of Scotland. As the town's population rapidly grew, so did its extent.

An entirely new town was built on the East bank of the River Cart. This, the Newtown of Paisley, was planned by James, Earl of Abercorn. His family owned most of the land where the new town was to be built. Where once stood the old Abbey gardens, new streets appeared. The Earl named these streets Cotton, Silk, Gauze and Mill in honour of the successful trades and manufactures of the town. In 1779, the Newtown could boast "upwards of twenty regularly formed and closely built streets". A contemporary described the scene, "The elegant appearances of the grand houses which are built in Gauze Street, strikes the attention of the travelling stranger. Most of these are three storeys high with doors and cornices ornamented with different orders".

Extract of 1822 map of Paisley, showing the Tontine's central location at the Newtown Cross.

The most impressive building of the Newtown was the Renfrewshire Tontine, built at the corner of Gauze Street and Bank Street. Paisley people were happy to note that this inn was one of the largest of its type in Scotland. It was built by the Earl of Abercorn at his own expense. He employed a London architect to give him the latest fashionable design. Work began in 1780 and, two years later, the building opened.

Its main three-storey, arcaded front faced Gauze Street. Over its principal portico was an antelope supporting the arms of the Earl of Abercorn, its patron. At the corner, was an elegant, pilastered bow-front, surmounted by a ballustraded, lead roof. Behind the bow-front on the ground floor, was a fashionable coffee room, where gentlemen of the town would gather to discuss business and keep up with the latest news and gossip. From this room, a grand geometry stair led up to the upper floors, where "thirty fine rooms all with fine fireplaces" could accommodate paying residents. In addition, there was a large hall, elegantly decorated and suitable for all kinds of functions. At the rear of the building, an enclosed yard held six coach houses, with stabling for twenty eight horses.

Soon, the inn became popular with Paisley gentry. The building was admirably suited for use, among other things, as a masonic hall. Its triangular shape and orientation suited the craft. In 1805, one of its earliest patrons was Renfrew County Kilwinning Lodge .

The large hall of the Abercorn Inn was put to other uses. It became the New Tontine Theatre. In 1824, the manager of the theatre, J.E. Byrne, brought the celebrated actor, Edmund Kean (of the Theatre Royal, Drury Lane), to appear in Paisley. Kean was regarded as the leading Shakespearian actor of his day. The cost of tickets was high. The manager's reason for the admission prices was, "The very great terms given to Mr Kean". Boxes cost 5/-,Pit 3/6d, Gallery 2/,... a small fortune in these days. However, such charges did not prevent wealthier Paisley drama lovers from attending.

On Kean's first Wednesday evening appearance as "Othello", the theatre was a sell-out. The manager put up a poster, "At the unanimous request of the overflowing audience who could not obtain admission to the theatre on Wednesday evening, Mr Byrne has succeeded in prevailing upon the celebrated actor to perform here ONE NIGHT MORE, being positively his last appearance".

When this picture was taken around 1900, the Tontine's popularity had waned.
The once grand coffee room had become a public house and the main building fronting
Gauze Street was turned into shops. (photo courtesy Paisley Museum)

The popularity of the Renfrewshire Tontine was to last into late Victorian times. Here, the Abercorn Football Club, who played at nearby East-End park, would hold their annual functions and dances. The 1870s saw Linside Cricket Club meet in the Abercorn Rooms to hold their annual dances. They would dance the night away with quadrilles, polkas and waltzes.

So respectable a place was the Abercorn Rooms, that even church congregational soirees gathered there. One soiree to welcome a new minister was so well attended that "The limits of the Abercorn Rooms were much too restricted for the crowd who considered it their duty to be present and the result was that many had to stand, after the tea was over."!

With the opening of the Town Hall in 1882, the popularity of the old inn began to wane. The once grand coffee room became a public house and the room above this became a newsboys' club room. The main building fronting Gauze Street was turned into shops. Around the the early part of this century, the porches with their pillars were removed to improve the breadth of the pavement.

In 1969, before it was demolished, the building held one last surprise. A large stone cistern, which reputedly dated from the old days of the nearby monastery, was unearthed in the cellar. This last relic of a notable Paisley building old can now be seen in Edinburgh, in the National Museum of Antiquities.

John Henning

John Henning, 1771-1851, from a portrait by R.S.Lauder.(courtesy SNPG Edinburgh).

If any man deserves a statue in Paisley's new pedestrian High Street it is John Henning, Paisley's forgotten genius, who was to achieve fame, but not fortune, as "a very ingenious modeller" and sculptor. In his day, the rich and famous of the land, including royalty, clamoured to have their portraits made by this man of working class origins from Paisley.

John Henning was born in Paisley in 1771, eldest son to Samuel, a talented master wright and architect-builder. The house where John was born is now the site of Paisley Central Library. John received his early education at the nearby Commercial School in Meeting House Lane, where he fondly remembered his old writing master, Ebenezer Macome, as "The man of whom I learned the value of application".

At the age of 13, John entered his father's joinery business, where he learned to draw plans and "began seriously to handle the hatchet, saw, plane and other implements of carpentry".

Henning's medallion portrait of The Duke of Wellington.

In 1799, two events took place which changed the humble joiner's life. He became engaged to Kate Sunter, who had agreed "to enter into co-partnership for life" and, later that year, they married. In his words they "were buckled together for life".

The second event changed John's working life completely. In Paisley, John and a friend saw a travelling exhibition, which included some wax busts. Immediately, John became inspired with the idea of making such small wax portraits himself. He set to work using one of his father's workmen, Woodrow, as the model. On completion of the wax portrait, which achieved a tolerable likeness, "Woodrow became clamourous for his own wax

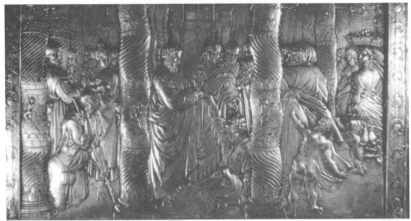

In 1821, Henning made this beautiful miniature plaque as a copy of a Raphael cartoon. The surface on which which Henning moulded the forms was only 5mm thick yet he achieved remarkable life-like forms and stunning linear perspectives. This was the genius of Henning!

ghost". As far as John was concerned, the result was not particularly successful and he would have given up his artistic efforts there and then. But his father's business was in decline and this forced John to seek some other means of livelyhood.

Soon, friends and acquaintances in Paisley begged John to capture their likeness in his delicate wax profiles. By 1800, John had agreed to make the likenesses of some Glasgow business men. Starting a new career so late in life, John was unsure of himself. He strode to Glasgow "with a perplexed mind, regretting the commissions he had undertaken", but, despite his own misgivings about his artistic talent, he proved to be a great success. He opened his first studio in Glasgow in 1801. His most important patron, the Duke of Hamilton, brought well-deserved recognition to Henning's first studio.

It was then suggested to Henning that he should move to Edinburgh, "where it is more a field for artists than Glasgow". Henning moved in 1801, "with fear and trembling", to the Athens of the North. His fears were soon put aside, as many of the leading lights in the capital flocked to his studio, including such famous men as James Watt and Sir Walter Scott. To improve his drawing skills, he was admitted to the Trustees Academy in Edinburgh. For a once humble Paisley joiner that was an achievement in itself! At this time, Henning perfected his technique in making portrait medallions in wax, plaster and glass enamel.

Soon Henning outgrew what Edinburgh had to offer and he was recommended to go to London. He arrived there in 1811, but was, at first, disappointed with the city and its inhabitants. Chance, however, led him to Burlington House, where the sight of the Elgin Marbles left Henning "so struck with these wonderful fragments", that he obtained permission from Lord Elgin "to draw and model from them".

Portrait medallion of Mrs Smith of George Square, Glasgow. This is typical of his highly-detailed portrait work .

Henning was to spend twelve long years drawing and making miniature restored plaster casts of the marble friezes. The delicate moulds to form the casts were painstakingly cut out of slate in reverse (intaglio), were two inches high and, when laid end to end, measured a total of thirty-three feet!

Henning gained little financial reward for his long labours, although he sold many original copies to the aristocracy. His work was ruthlessly pirated and copied as far away as Paris and Rome, but not a penny from abroad came his way.

During his years in London, Henning made portraits of various celebrities, including the Duke of Wellington, Sir Humphrey Davy, Thomas Telford, Mrs Sarah Siddons the actress, and a host of the London society. The highlight of his career came with sitters such as the Duke of Clarence (William IV) and Charlotte, the Princess of Wales.

In 1812, as the princess sat for her portrait, Henning, a true Paisley radical, attempted to interest her in books on Scottish dissent. Having read the books, she later told Henning, "I am not indulged with that kind of reading."!

The success of this royal portrait medallion led to orders from the pottery of Josiah Wedgwood. Wedgwood thought highly of Henning's intricate work and described him as a "very ingenious modeller."Besides, it made good business sense to use Henning's classical friezes to decorate the classical vases for which Wedgwood was renowned.

Henning obtained further commissions on a larger scale. He and his sons, John and Samuel, who were both talented sculptors and modellers, made the decorative friezes adorning important buildings in London and Manchester. In 1828, the Henning family produced their most famous and lovely work, the classical reliefs on the triple arches of Hyde Park Corner.

In his old age, Henning made one last attempt to get recognition and recompense for his original restored miniatures of the Elgin Marbles, but this too failed. He died in poverty in London, in 1851.

However, as an artist, he had been recognised during his life. Between 1821 and 1827, he exhibited at the Royal Academy in London and, in 1827, he was made an honorary member of the Royal Scottish Academy. In 1846, to honour one of her most famous sons, Paisley gave him the freedom of the burgh. His revered name ranks equally with Tannahill and Wilson in Paisley and yet there is no public memorial to this genius of a man.

Jessie Tennant

Portrait of Robert Tannahill who spurned his unfaithful sweetheart Jessie Tennant, the subject of one of his most famous songs, "Jessie, the Flower O' Dunblane".

Did Robert Tannahill, Paisley's famous weaver poet who met his untimely death in 1810, ever have a sweetheart? This question has often intrigued his admirers. It was generally supposed by the poet's closest friends that the only women in his life were the imaginary ones made famous in his songs. The poet was a shy and private man. But how could a man write so many beautiful love songs about women unless he, himself, had loved.

Was Tannahill's song "Jessie the Flower O' Dunblane" written for a real or an imagined woman? This question perplexed Paisley Buddies for many years. Sixty years after the poet's death, the search to find the real Jessie, if there was one, began.

On the face of it, it seemed a hopeless task. Various women residing in Dunblane claimed the honour. It appears one claimant was not a pretty sight as "she formed the counterpart of the pure creature of the poet's song". Other candidates proffered themselves, hoping to share in the fame of Tannahill's song. None succeeded in their spurious claims.

One man in Paisley pursued the truth with Victorian vigour. David Semple was the noted authority on the life of the poet. He discovered that Tannahill did in fact have a girlfriend. Her name was Jessie Tennant and she was, indeed, from Dunblane. She had come to Paisley to stay in John Street, not far from Tannahill's Queen Street cottage.

Jessie's friendship with the poet began in 1795. Tannahill courted this good-looking girl for three years, but not without some difficulty. Jessie complained to her friends that when she and Robert took walks in the surrounding country, he rarely spoke to her. It appeared that the poet was of a retiring, quiet nature and bashful in the extreme as far as ladies were concerned. Robert was inexperienced in the art of courtship, while Jessie was a pretty woman with a winning manner, not averse to flirting. However, the shy poet expressed his deep love for her in the way he knew best, in song. Jessie is lovingly described

TANNAHILL'S SONGS.

Jessie, the Flower o' Dumblane.

Music by R. A. Smith.

This beautiful song was first published in 1808 and is still popular today.

"Yet sweeter and fairer and dear to this bosom,
Is lovely young Jessie, the flower O' Dunblane".

During their courtship, Jessie would persuade a reluctant Tannahill to take her to local dances held in the Masonic Lodge in New Street. Robert had a bad leg and walked with a pronounced limp. He hated being on show and dancing embarrassed him. Jessie wanted Tannahill to take her to the Town's Annual Ball, one of the social events of the year, but he refused point blank. Jessie was then asked by a friend if he could take her to this grand occasion. Against his better judgement, Tannahill allowed his betrothed to go.

As the day of the ball arrived, Tannahill became restless and uneasy. That evening, he hid in Jessie's close to await her return from the ball. As Jessie and her escort said goodnight, he was horrified to see the man "plant a kiss on the ruby lips of the beautiful Jessie". To the jealous Tannahill, the "silver thread of love had snapped" .

That night, he crept back to his cottage, sat down and wrote a poem which he delivered to Jessie in the morning. The hurriedly written poem was far from being complimentary and had the ominous title "Fareweel". Tannahill's love for Jessie had gone and jealousy and anger prevailed. He did not spare his words,

A few yards from Tannahill's grave in Castlehead Church, lies the grave of Jessie.

"But when I knew thy plighted lips
Once to a rival's prest,
Love-smothered independence rose,
And spurn'd thee from my breast".

It was indeed a final 'fareweel' to Jessie. The two lovers were never reconciled. In 1798, Jessie married the rival of that fateful night. She lived until she was sixty-three, long out-living her one time love. She died at Orr Square in 1833, and was interred in the burial ground of the West Relief Church (Castlehead Parish Church).

Some of Jessie's children emigrated to Canada. It was from these Canadian grandchildren that proof came of Jessie's love affair with Tannahill. In 1874, the grandchildren revealed that they held the original, handwritten manuscript of the poem "Farweel" which their grandmother had received from the hands of the angry Robert Tannahill, that fateful morning in 1798. The mystery of the real "Jessie, the Flower O' Dunblane" had been solved.

Ironically, the two lovers now lie buried a few yards apart from each other, separated forever in death as in life.

Audubon meets Wilson

Portrait of Alexander Wilson 1776-1813. A radical poet and weaver in his home town who became one of the world's great naturalists.

In February 1810, Alexander Wilson, Paisley's famous exiled ornithologist, set out on yet another of his solo expeditions. In the company of his tame Carolina parrot and in his trusty skiff, which he had baptised "The Ornithologist", he sailed down the Ohio River in his quest to find new bird specimens. He hoped to include these new bird discoveries in the latest volumes of his his work "The American Ornithology". Two volumes had already been published. To prepare for his books, Wilson had spent many years traversing the vast tracks of America to observe and draw the huge range of native bird life.

Audubon's illustration of the Red-winged Blackbird (shown at the top) bore an uncanny resemblance to Wilson's much earlier portrayal of the same bird.

He arrived at Louisville, Kentucky, on 17th March after a voyage of 720 miles. He stayed in Louisville for seven days, to seek out subscribers to pay for further volumes of his work. Wilson dropped into various places if they seemed to hold promise of a subscription. By a strange coincidence, Wilson entered the store of John James Audubon, who was then an obscure merchant in this frontier town. Twenty one years later, Audubon would publish the world famous book "The Birds of America".

In later life, Audubon recalled the day when Wilson came into the store which Audubon ran with his partner Rosier. He remembered that Wilson had a long, rather hooked nose, keen eyes and prominent cheek bones. His dress was unusual for that part of America, as he wore a short coat, trousers and a waistcoat of grey cloth. Tucked under his arm were two large books. The visitor quickly stated his business, laid the books on the shop counter and explained about his study of ornithology. He then asked Audubon if he would care to subscribe to his work. A subscription would be $120, a fairly expensive outlay in those days.

Audubon leafed through the work without much comment and, taking a pen from the counter, was about to sign up when Rosier interrupted. He said," My dear Audubon, what induces you to subscribe to this work? Your drawings are certainly better and, again, you must know as much of the habits of American birds as this gentleman". Always easily flattered, Audubon laid down his pen.

Wilson, until that moment feeling safe in the uniqueness of his enterprise, was taken aback. He asked Audubon if, indeed, he had drawn many birds. Audubon reached for a large folio and proceeded to show his drawings to an astonished Wilson. Wilson was rather vexed and annoyed that Audubon's

After his traumatic meeting with Audubon, the downhearted Wilson parted with his pet Carolina Parrot, his favourite companion in his travels across America.

drawings were so skilled, yet he knew in his heart that his own drawings were more comprehensive in scale and more scientifically accurate.

Audubon claimed that he had a larger set of bird drawings than Wilson, but this claim was highly unlikely to be true. By 1810, the year the two first met, Wilson had travelled widely across America recording his birds. Audubon was, at this time, only a provincial, backwoodsman in Louisville. Also during his travels, Wilson had commissioned reliable agents throughout America, to act as bird scouts on his behalf. Audubon had no such helpers.

Two days after the historic meeting with Audubon, Wilson left Louisville, all the more determined to complete his mammoth task as quickly as possible. Wilson knew that sometime in the future Audubon would undoubtedly publish a book of his own. This fact worried Wilson and spurred him on to greater concentration in the completion of the final volumes of his "American Ornithology."

Before he Left Louisville, the slightly down-hearted Wilson parted with his pet parrot, sold his boat and took off southward on horseback to foray for more bird life. Between 1810 and 1813, Wilson worked incessantly, collecting more bird specimens, writing definitive descriptive texts of the birds and making coloured drawings, all to be included in the later volumes of his "American Ornithology."

Wilson's hard work paid off. He managed to complete most of his work and have it published some 21 years before Audubon. Wilson had drawn from life 320 birds of America, of which 39 were new to science. He was indeed the "Father of American Ornithology" and even had six birds named after him. Wilson's work had laid the foundation for Audubon. It is claimed that several of Audubon's bird illustrations in his

"Birds of America" were copied from Wilson's earlier work.

Today, the works of the rival ornithologists, Wilson's "American Ornithology" and Audubon's "Birds of America", are safely held in Paisley Library. The priceless books are the pride of Paisley. A statue of the famous Paisley ornithologist, who travelled alone through the American wilderness, stands in the grounds of Paisley Abbey.

Black Peter

When Peter Burnet, a black American, first arrived at the Tannahill family cottage in Queen Street, he must have turned a few heads.However, within an hour of meeting the Tannahills, Peter felt quite at home.

A flamboyant, colourful character called Peter Burnet arrived in Paisley in 1780. He was a stranger to the town, armed only with a letter of introduction to James Tannahill, the father of the poet. His appearance must have turned a few heads, because Peter Burnet was a black American, a rare sight in the Paisley of those days.

Peter Burnet had first been brought to Scotland to be employed as a valet to a rich Glasgow merchant. When the merchant's business failed, it was suggested to Peter that he should learn a trade if he wished to remain in Scotland. His old master sent him to seek work as a millwright with a George Tannahill in Kilmarnock.

However, when Peter arrived in Kilmarnock, George Tannahill convinced him that he would be better off in Paisley where he could learn the more prosperous art of weaving. Peter set out for Paisley bearing a letter of introduction to George's cousin, James Tannahill, the father of the Poet.

Peter made his way to the Tannahill family cottage in Queen Street and was spotted by one of James Tannahill's sons. "When I saw him first, and enquiring for my father's house, I imagined him to be the Black Prince of Kilmarnock. I had been sent on some errand and when I returned home Peter was sitting in my father's armchair, with all the family gathered round him, laughing at various stories". Within an hour, Peter felt quite at home.

An early painting of 'Tannahill's Hole'. The culvert to the left of the old canal is where Tannahill drowned in 1810. Black Peter was the man who recovered the body.

Peter was apprenticed to James Gibson, a weaver in West Street, but this did not work out. He was then sent to John Boag, where he became a fully-fledged weaver. Peter fell in love with John Boag's daughter, Peggy. He then set up his own loom and lodged with the Hutcheson family in Well Street.

As an independent, well-off Paisley weaver, Peter dressed in the latest fashions of the day. He wore a long black coat, a black velvet vest covered with gold spangles, nankeen breeches fastened at the knees with silver buckles, white thread stockings and steel shoe buckles. Lace ruffles adorned his breast cuffs. Underneath all the trappings stood a strong, well-built, muscular man about six feet tall. The only thing to distinguish from other weavers of the day, apart from the colour of his skin, was the tuft of hair on the crown of his head. Peter still believed in African mythology and that the tuft of hair would allow him to be lifted up to heaven when he died!

Peter became a well-loved figure in Paisley and thoroughly enjoyed its social life. He himself was an accomplished dancer. However, the merry life he led came to a sudden halt in 1788, when the weaving trade went through a severe depression. Peter took up his old occupation as a valet and moved to Edinburgh where his work took him into high society circles.

When the weaving trade in Paisley picked up, Peter returned to his adopted town. With his high earnings once again in full swing, he acquired many new companions in the social life of Paisley. He was often seen playing bowls in the newly-erected bowling alley at the head of West Street.

However, once again Peter's merry life was to receive a severe check when his landlord claimed that Peter owed him money. The claim was false, but Peter was imprisoned in the town's Tolbooth. To sustain him, the Tannahills and other friends sent him a bed and a supply of food. Peter was eventually freed from jail on taking an oath of poverty.

A later view of 'Tannahill's Hole' with Ferguslie Mill in the background.

He turned to the "star of his affections", Peggy Boag. She, in no uncertain fashion, told Peter that unless he changed his ways there would be no marriage between them. By this time Peter felt he had sown all his wild oats. He toned down his life-style and mixed with more sober companions. Peggy accepted his proposal and the two became man and wife. Sadly, Peggy and her first baby died during childbirth. Peter was distraught and inconsolable. He turned to the Tannahill family for consolation.

Time, however, revived his drooping spirits and Peter informed the Tannahills that he would take another wife. This time, he had decided to marry for money, not love. Peter had heard that there was a young mulatto girl in Beith, who had a fortune of £2000 at her disposal. Peter called upon her at her house, but returned to Paisley crestfallen. With a rueful face he shook his head and said "It will not do". Peter had been cured of monetary love.

He then began to tell his friends that "he would bring home a wife, one of the finest girls he ever saw". This, Peter claimed, would astonish the natives of Paisley. At length he did bring home a wife from Glasgow, "one of the prettiest young creatures you could see amongst a thousand". Peter lived happily with his new wife. Trade was good. He took one of the best tradesmen's houses in Paisley and fitted it out with excellent furniture. Three children soon followed. Later, his wife became ill and died of consumption. Peter was once again a widower. Only one child of this marriage survived into adulthood.

Peter married a third time and lived for many years in Maxwelton Street. He then moved to the other end of the town, became ill and was long confined to his bed. His third wife died. By 1841, Peter was an old man and through failing eyesight could no longer work. John Parkhill, one of Peter's friends, wrote a biography of Peter's life. He gave the book to Peter to sell, hoping that the modest profit it might make would alleviate the "distressing circumstances in which he was placed". Peter Burnet died in 1847, at the ripe old age of eighty-six. He is best remembered in Paisley's story as the man who took the dead body of his friend, the poet Robert Tannahill, from the Candren Burn, where he had committed suicide.

Hutcheson's Charity School

Hutcheson's Charity School in Oakshaw, built not a stone's throw away from the burial place of its generous founder, Margaret Hutcheson.

On the west wall of the graveyard of the old High Church, a tombstone from times past has a touching inscription and a timely reminder of human mortality.

"This is the burying place of John Park and Margaret Hutcheson, his wife, 1789.
By faith a man enjoys his maker;
By love his neighbours,
And by contentment himself,
Remember, man, as thou go'st by,
As thou art now, so once was I;
As I am now, so thou must be;
Therefore, prepare to follow me."

In 1805, Hutchison's Charity School moved to a room in the 'Wee Steeple' in Paisley High Street. With the demolition of this building in 1807, the pupils moved into the nearby meeting house owned by the 'Pen Folk'.

John Park and Margaret Hutcheson were a humble, but happy, married couple. Although he had been born in the parish of Houston and she in the parish of Govan, they resided in Paisley for the greater part of their lives. John Park was a labourer and gardener, so the family income was poor. However, their fortune was soon to change.

Margaret had a brother, James, who had emigrated and settled in St John's on the island of Antigua. He was a tailor to trade and, over the years, he had built a substantial business and amassed a large fortune. With his money, he had bought a large estate and plantation. His sister, Margaret was his next of kin. When her brother died, she inherited a sum of more than £20,000! In those days, it must have been the equivalent of winning the national lottery! Overnight, the lives of John Park and Margaret Hutcheson changed. In Paisley, never a town to ignore money, the couple became a financial institution.

Despite their large fortune, they acted with prudence. They were eminently kind to the poor and charitable to friends and relations by giving and lending money. Their donations were numerous. £100 was given to the Ladies' Hospital. Kirk Sessions of Paisley and Houston received considerable sums of money from the pious couple. Included in other donations was money to support a public dispensary in Paisley. Old people in the town with the name of Park or Hutcheson were to receive support. Money to support the institution of a Sunday School in the town was liberally given.

John and Margaret also bought a considerable amount of property in Paisley. They bought a "dwelling house, barn and pertinents" at St James Street. They also purchased eight acres of common land in Moss Street, at a cost of £440.

Money continued to flow into John and Margaret's coffers. From the estate in Antigua, Margaret received regular sums of £1100 as mortgage payments from the business man who had purchased her brother's plantation.

The couple had no family and all their vast fortune was bequeathed to a large number of legatees. Margaret Hutcheson died in 1795, aged 70, followed by her husband two years later.

Two years before she died, Margaret had made provision to set aside £1500 "as a fund for erecting, establishing and endowing a Charity School in the town of Paisley, to be called Hutcheson's Charity School". Its purpose was to instruct poor orphans or the children of poor parents residing in Paisley. The children were to be taught how to read and write, to be given the "common rules of arithmetic" and taught the "principles of Christian religion,"all under the supervision of "proper teachers".

In 1804, the first "proper teacher "appointed was a Mrs Sharp and the first school began in a temporary room in Paisley High Street. The school had 44 day pupils and 40 evening pupils. The following year, the scholars moved to larger premises at the 'Wee Steeple' or Almshouse. With the demolition of this building in 1807, pupils were transferred to a nearby meeting house owned by the 'Pen Folk' or Baptists. At this time, a most welcome donation to the school funds was given by a Mr Carswell, who stipulated that "there would be a decided preference to all such children bearing the name of Carswell". But the number applying for entry with that name should not exceed ten!

By good management of Margaret Hutcheson's original endowment, followed by other donations over the years, the school proved very successful. New premises were urgently required to house the growing number of pupils. A site was bought for £100 in 1818, at the corner of 'Pen Lane' and Oakshaw Street and, there, a new school was erected in 1822. The new building was designed in a simple, unpretentious, classical manner by the local architect Mr Vallance, who received 12 guineas as his fee. The school could now accommodate 250 pupils. The splendid new building now effactually promoted the school's standing in Paisley. During a brief episode in 1832, the school rooms were used as a temporary cholera hospital and besieged by an angry mob taking part in Paisley's infamous "cholera riots". But the school survived and continued to give basic education to the poorer classes of the town.

In 1883, the school rules were changed. Rule No 6 stated that "the corporal punishment of the children be limited to stripes with a tawse, only on the palms of the hands"! The children, however, had not many years left to suffer the dreaded tawse at Hutcheson's Charity School, as it was finally closed in 1889. The old building now forms part of the halls of Oakshaw Trinity Church and features in the Paisley Heritage Trail.

John Orr

View of John Orr's Underwood Cotton Mill, (which once stood opposite St James Church) where some of his aggrieved workers regarded their employer as operating "a dark satanic mill" and set out to kill him.

On the evening of Saturday 16th December, 1820, the streets of Paisley were buzzing with the news of an attempted murder. Someone had attempted to assassinate Mr John Orr, one of the town's important cotton mill owners. John Orr was a partner in the Underwood Cotton Mill owned by the influential Orr family. Being a mill owner at this time had its difficulties. Orr and other local mill owners had reduced their workers' wages earlier that year and Orr's workers had gone on strike to try and force him to maintain their previous wages. Orr became the hated target of his discontented workers and had narrowly missed death on a previous occasion when he was shot at outside his own house.

It was while taking late evening supper at his Uncle William's house in Causeyside, that another attempt on his life was made. Orr was informed by his uncle's housekeeper that two men wished to speak to him at the front door. The two rough-looking men were invited into the parlour by the housekeeper, but declined the invitation, saying that their business was urgent.

Orr had scarcely reached the street door, when two loaded pistols were discharged at him. Miraculously, he was not hit. Outside in the street, the two gunmen and their two accomplices instantly fled. Their diabolical plan to kill John Orr had failed and they ran off in the direction of Glasgow. In their panic, they stopped at the Paisley Tollhouse on Glasgow Road, hoping to disappear into the cover of one of its public rooms.

An old tollhouse once stood at the junction of Glasgow Road and Incle Street. Here, in 1820, Orr's attackers concealed themselves. In Victorian times, a new tollhouse replaced the old. It appears on the right of the picture, and is sadly, long gone.

The four men were duly ushered in to a room by a rather suspicious maid servant. It was late in the evening for travellers and she was frightened by their rough appearance. She instantly informed her master and his wife that "robbers were in the house". Through a hole in the door, all three saw the ruffians place two pistols on the table. It was noticed that one of them was wearing a white neckcloth to disguise his face. In his panic and confusion, he had forgotten to take it off and destroy it.

It is not recorded exactly what happened next, but, some days later, when a reward of 20 guineas was offered for the capture of the criminals, they were soon apprehended and taken into custody. It transpired that two of the men involved in the case, Cameron and Lafferty, had worked for John Orr at his Underwood Mills as cotton spinners. Cameron had, indeed, worked at the mill only two days before the shooting.

At their trial in the High Court in Edinburgh, the court heard that, a few days before the shooting, the four had had met in O'Donnell's Pub in Causeyside and had hatched a plan to assassinate their employer. It was decided that one of them would be disguised in a borrowed great coat and wear a white neckcloth to hide his face. He would then hand over a letter to John Orr. As Orr opened the letter, two pistols would be fired at him. The clothes would be disposed of after the shooting had taken place.

At the top of Well Street, each of the prisoners received 15 lashes, was jailed and sent for transportation. Well Street, of course, has changed a lot since then...

The court found the case against Lafferty not proven, but Cameron and the other two men were found guilty. They were sentenced to be publicly whipped through the streets of Paisley and then to be transported for life. The sentence was to be carried out on April 1821.

This public event brought huge crowds into Paisley to witness the severe punishment for attempted assassination and every window overlooking the route of the procession was filled with eager spectators. Outside the jail, the Paisley Rifle Corps stood to arms to ward off the curious crowds.

The convicts were brought out of the jail and tied by the hands to a cart which was escorted by a troop of dragoons and a detachment of foot. Behind the cart marched local sheriffs and their attendant officers accompanied by the Paisley Police Force. The culprits were to be whipped at various stopping points in the town. The man selected to perform this gruesome task was the public executioner, hired for the day from Glasgow.

The whippings took place at the top of Well Street, New Street, the Cross, Moss Street and finally in New Sneddon Street. At these places, each prisoner received fifteen lashes, a total of seventy-five. The crowd of onlookers, though immense, proved orderly and deadly silent as they witnessed the punishments. The prisoners were then returned to jail and sent for transportation for life.

Mr John Orr of Underwood Mills was elected Provost in 1832. Besides being the chief dignitary of the burgh, he was also a justice of the peace for the county and filled many other offices of trust in the town. He had survived two attempts on his life and died on a business trip to Liverpool in 1841, aged 57. He lies buried in the High Church Yard.

Duncan Henderson

Cobbett's Dwarf Indian Seed Corn
FOR SALE.

As the time for committing the Seed of this highly valuable, most productive, and beautiful Plant to the Ground, is at hand, the Subscriber intimates, that he has a quantity of Cobbett's rearing, from his Farm at Barn Elm, Crop 1831. The Subscriber has also a part of his own Seed, grown last Year at Cowieston, from the Plants visited and so much admired by many thousands. From personal observations made by him, on examining various plots in Paisley and its neighbourhood, he has been led to conclude, that the latter end of April, or beginning of May, is the most proper time for planting the Seed in the West of Scotland. Correspondents in the Country are therefore requested to avail themselves of the present notice, by making an early application. The Subscriber has devoted his attention to the introduction of this Plant into Scotland, for the last three Years, under a firm conviction that its cultivation will be, from its highly nutritive qualities, very beneficial to all classes of the community. He recommends a light sandy soil, or fine loam; the drills to be three feet asunder, and eight inches betwixt each seed; to be set with plenty of horse, cow, or pig's dung, well rotted; as the plants get up, to be well hoed betwixt the rows, and the earth drawn up to the roots—by paying attention to these simple directions, a fair crop may be anticipated. He had from 3 to 5 ears on each plant, so that some of them produced nine-hundred fold.

Ears 6d. each, or 4d. per ounce.

DUNCAN HENDERSON.

Cowieston, April 18, 1832.

Neilson & Hay, Printers.

Advertising handbill for Cobbett's Dwarf Indian Seed Corn.
Printed in Paisley in 1832 for Duncan Henderson.

Paisley Florist Society, which was founded in 1782, is the oldest in Scotland. Its original members were mostly handloom weavers and specialised in growing auriculas, carnations and pinks.

In the 18th and 19th century, Paisley weavers were renowned for developing a variety of laced pinks. One possible survivor of the famous "Paisley Pinks" still grown today is the "Paisley Gem".

In the history of horticulture, Paisley's reputation is quite remarkable. One man who did much to enhance this reputation was Duncan Henderson. For many years, Henderson was a grocer and spirit dealer. His shop was in a one-storey, thatched building at the south end of Maxwelton Street, facing Newton Street. This part of Paisley was known in the 19th Century, as Cowieston. High rise flats now occupy the site.

In 1831, Duncan Henderson successfully grew in his garden, "Cobbett's Corn". We now know this as "corn on the cob". This was the first time people in Paisley had seen this strange American crop growing and it was the first time it had ever been grown in Scotland. Thousands of people came to Paisley to admire the new plants, buy seed and learn how to cultivate it.

Duncan Henderson had spent three years introducing this new crop to Scotland. He had first acquired corn seed from Barn Elm Farm in England, whose owner was the famous political journalist, William Cobbett. Cobbett was a champion of the poor and the uncompromising advocate of Radicalism.

Portrait of William Cobbett (1762-1835)
English political journalist who
campaigned for social, economic reform.
Author of "Weekly Political Register" and
"Rural Rides", visited Paisley in 1832.

His "Weekly Political Register" newspaper campaigned for much needed, social economic reform in Great Britain.

It was no wonder that he was a popular man in Paisley, as the Paisley weavers were radical to a man and were familiar with Cobbett's works and ideas.

To Duncan Henderson, Cobbett was a hero, so it was not surprising that he became a zealous follower. In becoming Cobbett's agent in Scotland for "Cobbett's Corn", he followed his master's footsteps in advocating the introduction of this crop "with its highly nutritious qualities" and which would be "beneficial to all classes of the community".

When William Cobbett made a tour of Scotland in 1832, he stayed in Paisley for four days. He was the guest at a house in Garthland Place, home of a local cloth merchant Archibald Stewart. During this stay, Cobbett delivered two public lectures and "astonished all parties with his shrewd and good natured eloquence". He was also honoured with a public dinner in the Saracen Head Inn, at Paisley Cross.

William Cobbett visited several people in the town, but, sadly, his greatest admirer, Duncan Henderson had just died. In his account of his tour of Scotland, published in 1833, Cobbett wrote:

"On the same day, when I expected to go and see Mr Henderson, who from his attachment to me, or rather to my writings, had taken so much pains to cultivate my corn, I was informed that I had to see his widow, for that he had died on the day of my first arrival in Glasgow.

As a mark of my respect for the memory of so worthy a man, a man of so much public spirit and so justly beloved, I went to see Mrs Henderson, at which she was very much pleased; and she showed me a letter written by myself to her late husband, on which she had set so much value as to have it framed and hung up as a picture. Not to see him, and, still more, to find that he was dead, really cast a damp over my pleasures at Paisley, though at no place where I have ever been in my life was I ever received with more cordiality, nor was my reception anywhere ever accompanied with circumstances better calculated to leave lasting impressions of gratitude on my mind".

PRIZES

PROPOSED TO BE AWARDED BY THE

PAISLEY HORTICULTURAL SOCIETY,

For 1834.

THE first Meeting for Competition, will be held on the first Thursday of July, within the Saracen's Head Inn, Articles to be presented betwixt 11 and 12 o'clock A. M., when two Prizes will be awarded for each of the following Articles :—

1. For the Three best Heads Caulliflower.
2. For the Six best early Horn Carrots.
3. For the Three best Heads Early Cabbage.
4. For the Twelve best Yellow Turnips.
5. For the Three largest and best Heads Curled Parsley.
6. For the best Three Dozen Pod Beans.
7. For the Two best Cucumbers.
8. For the Fifty best Strawberries.
9. For the Twelve best species of Hardy Perennial Flowers, as a Bouquet.

THE Second and General Meeting will be held on the second Thursday of September, at the same place : Articles to be presented betwixt 11 and 12 o'clock, when two Prizes will be awarded for each of the following Articles :—

10. For the Three best Heads Savoys.
11. For the Three best Heads Brocolie.
12. For the Three best Red Beet.
13. For the Six best Carrots.
14. For the Six best Heads Cellary.
15. For the Twelve best Apples, Four Varieties, Three of each.
16. For the Twelve best Pears, Four Varieties, Three of each.
17. For the Six best Varieties Double Dahlias, (Georginia.)
18. For the Twelve best Species of Annuals from the open Ground, put up as a Bouquet.

For any Flower, Fruit, or Vegetable of superior merit, either as a Variety or improved mode of Cultivation, One or more Prizes.

Articles presented for Competition, must be Cleaned and Prepared as for the Market.

Advertising handbill for Paisley Horticultural Society dated 1834. It would appear that growing prize vegetables in Paisley was more popular than cultivating Cobbett's Corn!

Duncan Henderson had died on 17th October 1832, six days before his hero, Cobbett, arrived in Paisley. Henderson had hoped that this highly nutritious new cereal, Indian Maize, could be grown in Scotland to feed the poor. He did not realise that it would not grow successfully in our cold, northerly climate. But, still, to him goes the honour of being first to try one of the new crops which would in the future, revolutionise farming. And all this in a Paisley backyard!

Only in 1854, did "Cobbett's corn" return to Paisley in a big way. But this time, many tons of corn grain were imported to the town from America, processed and marketed as Brown and Polson's "Patent Cornflour". ....but that is another story!

Paisley characters

This view, drawn in 1825, shows Paisley as a large and prosperous town. However, the town's infrastructure could not cope with the huge influx of immigrant workers, some of whom fell by the wayside to become poor vagrants, street hawkers and 'characters'. (courtesy Paisley Museum)

Paisley was always a colourful town full of characters. Even Paisley shopkeepers' signs during the 18th and 19th centuries were not without a sense of humour. One Paisley man, John McLean, who owned a public house at Townhead had a sign painted above the door which read:

"The reason that this sign stands here, I sell good Whiskey, Ale and Beer".
Not to be outdone, another publican's sign in Storie Street read:
"Whiskey and Ale are sold in here, and Porter too, by Robert Speir".
Over a cook's shop At Townhead:
"Pay today, and tomorrow for nothing!"

Barney Keir who was a chimney sweep by profession was, by all accounts, a real Paisley character. He conducted his black, sooty business from a building at 69 High Street. At that time in the early 1800s, this address was regarded as one of the wildest places in Paisley. It was known locally as the "Goosedubs" and teemed with vagrants and beggars. In 1804, Barney Keir erected a sign over his chimney sweep shop, advertising his services to the Paisley public:

DAFT SANDY

JAMIE BLUE.

Lang Tam, a wandering imbecile who received pennies from coach passengers, by giving them a gentle look. Daft Sandy, with outstretched hand, would say, "I'm daft man, gi'es a bawbee". Jamie Blue, who sold cheap literature, was a street singer and wrote poetry of sorts during election times. (courtesy Paisley Museum)

"Who lives here? Who do you think?
Barney Keir who loves a drink,
He loves a drink, I'll tell you why,
Barney Keir is often dry.
He sweeps chimneys and cleans smoke jacks;
And if your chimney goes on fire
He'll put it out to your desire.
CHIMNEY SWEEPER AND SOOT MERCHANT".

In Paisley, until about 1827, chimneys were swept by climbing boys. One Paisley writer stated, "We have seen small black urchins that could scarcely crawl along the street, creep up the vent with brush in hand to sweep the foul funnel. It was a cruel operation and little orphan boys were cruelly used by their masters. They sometimes stuck in the narrow vents and, on two occasions, we saw boys nearly suffocated dug out of walls".

Whether chimney sweep Barney Keir was a cruel master or not we shall never know, but he became such a well-known character in Paisley that, for many years after, a chimney sweep was called a "Barney Keir". Barney moved his sign and his lodgings farther along High Street to "Roperie Close" and lived there until he was an old man, walking about the town with crutches.

"Roperie Close"was better known in Paisley as "Little Hell". It was occupied by some unsavoury characters. One poor soul who lived here was Johnnie Flint. His house was a miserable hovel situated at the old West Port of the town, near what is now called Orr Square. Johnnie was typical of the many street pedlars or hawkers forced through abject poverty to trade their simple wares in the narrow streets and wynds of Paisley.

In appearance, Johnnie Flint was a dwarf of a figure. He had an uncouth look and walked with a decided wiggle. He also suffered great difficulty in speaking. To earn a meagre living, he sometimes delivered sand and, on other occasions, exchanged people's cast-off rags for earthenware plates and bowls. As he trundled his one-wheeled barrow through the streets of Paisley, he would cry out, "Plates and bowls for old rags!" Thoughtless young boys would tease and plague him and would cruelly mimic his cry. Although he was a pitiful sight and abjectly poor, Johnnie chose not to live off charity.

Tannahill, the poet, witnessed for himself the cruel taunts poor Johnnie had to suffer and, out of sympathy, wrote a poem called the "Bowlman's Remonstrance". This was first published in 1806:

"Thro' Winter's cold and Summer's heat,
I earn my scanty fare;
From morn till night, along the street
I cry my earthen ware."

Tannahill reminded his Paisley contemporaries not to scorn the likes of Johnnie Flint with his diminutive stature, uncouth appearance and awkward walk:

"The potter moulds the passive clay,
To all the forms you see,
And that same Pow'r that formed you
Hath likewise fashion'd me".

Tannahill also added a touching footnote to his poem in defence of Johnnie Flint: "When decrepitude incapacitates a brother of humanity from gaining subsistence by any of the less dishonourable callings, and when he possesses that independency of soul which disdains living on charity, it is certainly refinement in barbarity to hurt the feelings of such a one".

Another well-known character in Tannahill's time was a street beggar called "Daft Sandy". Unlike Johnnie Flint, he did live off the charity of others. He would stand at Paisley Cross and frequently approach the passengers arriving and departing in horse drawn coaches. With outstretched hands he would utter the words, "I'm daft man. Gie'sa bawbee!" Daft Sandy lived in the Saucel area of town and became so well-known as a town character that his portrait was engraved by a local printer and sold in the streets of Paisley.

Thomas Burnside

Portrait of Thomas Burnside (1822- 1879)

During the 1860s, Paisley was described as a remarkable place, one of the most remarkable in Scotland. The writer of these remarks was referring not to the physical appearance of the town, but to its poets. Paisley, said the writer, was the "abode of poetical inspiration and the favourite seat of the muses, where Apollo sits at the loom earning eighteen shillings a week". He also added "There is perhaps a greater number of poets living and breathing in this little town, than in the whole of England."

Paisley had been described as an 'nest of singing birds', where many had composed verses and where a surprising number had managed to have their works published.

One such poet was Thomas Burnside, who was born in the town in 1822. His father, Alexander, earned a living making reeds for the Paisley weaving trade. Thomas was brought up 'in frugal circumstances and nurtured in hardship'. He did not even have the advantage of a common school education. Like a lot of poor Paisley children, he was sent to work as a drawboy to a local weaver when only seven. At sixteen, he became an apprentice weaver.

When a fully-fledged weaver, Thomas was sent to stay and work for his uncle in Dunfermline. One evening while he was in bed, Thomas overheard a heated argument between his uncle and aunt concerning himself. It appeared that the aunt did not take kindly to her nephew's presence. Deeply offended,

Like so many Paisley boys, Thomas Burnside started life as a drawboy when only seven years old. At sixteen, he became a fully fledged weaver.

Thomas slipped out of their house while they were asleep. After wandering about for some time and becoming ill in the process, he arrived at his sister's house in Glasgow almost destitute and penniless. He found refuge and rest under his sister's care and soon his health recovered.

In 1843, he married a Margaret Marshall, whose worldly circumstances were no better than his own. That year, due to a severe depression in the weaving trade, Paisley was declared bankrupt. Work in Paisley was 'so ill to be got', that Thomas left. He managed to get employment in the village of Balfron and remained there for three years. Then he found occasional employment in Glasgow, working sometimes as a mill hand or as a weaver.

When the depression in Paisley was over, Thomas returned to his home town and managed to get employment as a factory weaver with one of the town's leading shawl manufacturers, David Speirs and Co. It was during this period that his eyesight became less keen and he was forced to forsake such detailed work. With the little savings he had gathered, he opened a small shop and stocked it as a circulating library. However, this failed after two years and he was forced to go back to the loom.

It was while sitting at the loom, that Thomas began to think deeply on the various ills of life and the difficulty of working one's way through them. But he always remained undaunted and cheerful. At the age of forty-three, he found solace in writing verses. When writing to his only son in Ardrossan, the thought struck him that he might, like Tannahill whose works were familiar to him, try and put his thoughts to rhyme.

Although his poems were written primarily to please himself, others in the town took notice. Burnside did not place a high estimate on his poems and regarded them as only reflecting some aspects of the community in which he lived. But his poems on the state of the weaving trade were witty and found a ready readership among his fellow weavers. His poem, 'Voice from the Workshop', proved popular among the aggrieved weavers.

"Then why should we labour for pittance so small,
While the rich have their thousands a year,
And a small kitchen serve us for bedroom and all,
While they their proud mansions uprear?
And why should the wealthy have power to oppress,
And use working men as their tools,
When true honest Union would bring us redress,
If we only abide by its rules?"

Thomas Burnside, always the radical, joined in another fight. He joined a temperance society, the Good Templars, for during his life he had seen the misery that drink brought to many a weaver and his family. At meetings, he would often sing his own songs and attract large crowds. His song, 'Never drink onything stronger than tea', was a favourite.

"Noo frien's haud yer tongue, an I'll sing ye a sang,
At least I will try 't, an dae a' that a' can;
An the pith o' my sang is a counsel to you,
For aye to keep sober whatever you do.
Aye to keep sober, aye to keep sober,
An never drink onything stronger than tea."

On one occasion he addressed a poem to a local blacksmith, Robert Pattison, who had failed to return a lock sent in for repair ten months previously.

"So Robin then withoot delay,
Send back the lock this very day,
As hale as when I saw ye tak it,
An' for the key, ye needna mak' it,
There's men in Paisley good an' true,
Can mak' a key as good as you;
May Clootie tak' ye for his ain,
If job ye get from me again."

Burnside considered that his poetical legs were never strong enough to climb the steep and rugged hill of Parnassus, but had to content himself with gathering the crumbs scattered round its base. Despite such modesty, some of his poems were published in the Paisley and Renfrewshire Gazette and in popular periodicals. Thomas Burnside was always popular in Paisley. Sadly, his poems were not published in book form until a year after his death. He died in 1879, aged 57.

Old Smithhills

The old tenement at No 17 Old Smithhills with wine and spirit vaults on the ground floor. Notice the unrestored North transept of Paisley Abbey on the left and Abbey Close to the right. Many of the buildings in this street were moved to make way for the Town Hall.

Robert Russell who was one of Paisley's earliest photographers, captured this scene of old Paisley in the early 1860s. It was taken to record what was considered to be a good specimen of a Paisley tenement built in 1763. This photographic record is all the more important as it captured for future generations of Paisley Buddies a building designed by Bailie John Whyte. Whyte was Paisley's most talented architect of the 18th Century. He was responsible for the design of some of the town's most important public buildings such as the Tolbooth and the Flesh Market. These have long since been demolished and Whyte's only remaining work is the old High Church at Oakshaw.

This historic photograph shows a large, three-storey tenement with attic dormer windows. It stood at the corner of Abbey Close and Smithhills. The ground floor was used as a public inn. Its design shows all the hallmarks of architect Whyte. Its fine proportions display the care and attention that Whyte gave to all his plans.

The man who built what was considered to be one of the most stylish residences in Paisley was Robert Buchanan. As soon as the tenement was completed, Buchanan sold off the flats to eager buyers.

Over a period of years, these desirable flats saw various owners come and go. The building was mainly occupied by the affluent middle classes, including many from the legal profession, lawyers, Town Clerks, and even Writers to the Signet.

The quoined gable of the old tenement leads in to Abbey Close. In 1873, all the tenements on the left hand side were demolished as part of a street widening programme. Notice the West gable of Paisley Abbey in the background.

In 1833, one flat was taken up by John Wilson, who was a well-known spirit merchant in Paisley. However, his stay was brief. In 1835, while he was aboard the steamship "Earl Grey" moored at Greenock Harbour, the ship's boiler burst. The exploding boiler sheared off the upper deck where Wilson and several others were standing. Wilson was killed in an instant. His tombstone describing his horrific, sudden death can be seen to this day within Paisley Abbey.

William Hector.

Coincidentally, a few years later a sign was erected above the public house on the ground floor. The painted sign read "The Earl Grey Inn". The new landlord, Duncan McMillan, named his inn after the Prime Minister of the day. The wags of Paisley instantly dubbed him "Earl Grey", since he thought himself as important as the real Earl!

In 1802, William Hector was born in one of the flats. He rose to become Sheriff Clerk for Renfrewshire and a keen amateur historian. William Hector left a wonderful legacy in his books on local history and was one of the main movers in re-establishing the Paisley Burns Club, which had been in abeyance for many years.

Another occupant of this fine building was Robert Wilson, a partner in the Paisley engineering firm of Hanna, Donald and Wilson. This company was world famous in its day for constructing large bridges, gasometers and building iron ships.

However, time was running out for the old building. The council, in their wisdom, decided in 1873 that all the buildings ranging from Smithhills and down the East side of Abbey Close had to be demolished. This tragically involved taking down part of the mediaeval cloister wing of the old abbey. All this was done in the name of progress to widen Abbey Close and give a better view of the abbey.

When the old tenement building was finally demolished it held a last surprise. As the workmen carefully removed the stonework, they discovered that the lintels above the windows were made of old, solid oak timber. They bore the marks of the skilled carpenter who had first made them. They appeared to have been beams or part of the roof structure of a much older building. In those days, it was common practice among builders to re-use old material, where possible, on new work.

To make way for Buchanan's tenement, the previous building on the site had been demolished. It had been the "Stately Yett House" or gatehouse of Paisley Abbey, built by Abbot Tervas in the 15th century. David Semple, the noted Paisley historian of the time, said, "I have not the least doubt that these oak lintels, from the strength and squaring of the timber came from the Stately Yett House connected with the abbey". The old lintels are now irretrievably lost like the mediaeval gatehouse, and Bailie Whyte and Robert Buchanan's building in Smithhills.

Patrick Brewster

Patrick Brewster's statue at Woodside Cemetery, erected in 1863. Paisley's first public monument to a well loved and respected public figure.

At Woodside Cemetery, a few years ago, the memory of a forgotten Paisley prophet was resurrected. In the shadow of Patrick Brewster's statue, the launch of a book about him took place. The book was called "Patrick Brewster"-and it was co-authored by John Murphy and Robbie Moffat. This was the long-awaited, first book to be written about the radical Paisley minister. So who was Patrick Brewster and what did he do in Paisley to merit a fine statue in Woodside Cemetery?

Was he a famous preacher? Was he a politician? Was he a philanthropist? Patrick Brewster was all of these things and much more. No reference can be made to the struggle for political reform and freedom of speech, in the 19th Century, without the mention of Brewster's name.

In 1818, he was appointed assistant minister at Paisley Abbey. Brewster was noted for the vigour and emotion of his sermons. This brilliant, charismatic young man with a powerful voice and shock of auburn hair, which impressed the ladies of the congregation, was the perfect choice for Paisley's oldest established church.

Sundays in Paisley, at this time, brought a riot of bells, from churches of many religious persuasions, each competing for worshippers. No single church claimed ascendancy over any one group. However, although Paisley 'had religion', it was also a place which had areas of poverty and drunken squalor. The town was seething with political unrest. It was in this atmosphere, in 1823, that the minister of Paisley Abbey died and his young assistant, Patrick Brewster, was offered the vacancy. Brewster insisted that he, his wife and children be given a new manse, as the old manse situated in Lawn Street was in a state of dilapidation. As this was not forthcoming from the church, Brewster refused to take up the appointment. This made him unpopular with the church authorities for turning down one of Scotland's premier charges. Much to his chagrin and anger, Brewster discovered that the minister who filled the vacancy did get a new manse!

This episode showed Brewster that the church was not even-handed in its dealings. He had been wounded by the aristocracy and its system of patronage and control in the church, so he turned his attentions to the unenfranchised worker's struggle for political and social reform. A good example was his support of the nearby Nitshill miners, for whom he ran evening education classes. Although he, himself, was not a 'radical', Brewster gave moral support and sympathy to the Paisley weavers, who were being harassed by government cavalry in the town's streets for their Radical activities. This was the time of early trade unionism, political intrigue and reform. Paisley had seen mass demonstrations at Meikleriggs Moor, cavalry charges down the High Street, public riots and trials for treason. A provisional 'secret army' among the working classes was ready to overthrow the government.

Such were Brewster's beliefs in equality and freedom of religion that, in 1829, he, a minister of the Church of Scotland, signed a petition in favour of the Catholic Emancipation Bill! That went down like a bomb with the church authorities!

Brewster had caught the political fever of the times. In 1835, he took part in a public dinner held in Glasgow to honour Daniel O' Connell MP. O'Connell advocated the dis-establishment of the Protestant Church in Ireland and Irish independence. Brewster drove with O'Connell in an open carriage to Paisley. There, they attended a public meeting in the Low Church, New Street (Paisley Arts Centre) to honour O'Connell. Paisley Presbytery then accused Brewster of 'entering a church with a Catholic'. The Paisley Advertiser newspaper accused him of being in favour of the 'Extirpation of the Protestant Church'. One church minister's condemnation of Brewster's part in the whole affair stated, "It was lamentable to think that men whose religious principles, they could not call into question, should have countenanced and united themselves with the emissary of the man of sin"! Brewster's replied to his 'bad press' with the following, "Had Mr O'Connell been a Conservative, had he come amongst us in the shape of a Catholic or a Protestant Peer, my present assailants would be my defenders". He was censured by Paisley Presbytery for his association with O'Connell, but had the support of his church congregation.

Although Brewster held extreme Chartist views, he was opposed to the use of force, preferring to use moral persuasion. O'Connell, on the other hand, advocated the use of violent physical force. Both men, however, did agree that socio-political reform was necessary in the country. So, a public debate between the two men was organised to take place in Paisley. The year was 1841. The venue for their confrontation, was a field in Abercorn Street. Temporary hustings were erected and hundreds gathered to hear the debate. Which was to be the best way to achieve the Chartist aims of the right to vote for all men, secret ballot elections, equal electoral districts, annual parliaments and the abolition of property qualifications for MP's. Would it be force or persuasion?

Portrait of Daniel O'Connell M.P. (1775-1847).

After the debate, the people in the crowd voted by dividing into two groups. Both Brewster and O'Connell claimed victory. O'Connell even climbed a tree to have a better view of the crowd! However, the matter of using physical force or moral force had not been resolved.

Once again, Brewster was accused by his church of consorting with Chartist insurrectionists. He fuelled further speculation by preaching "Chartist sermons" in the Abbey Church. He was accused by the church authorities of "irritating the poor against the rich" by his sermons. The General Assembly asked him to hand over the manuscripts of these "corrupting works", but, instead, he fearlessly preached them again!

In 1842, Brewster was charged with libel by his patron, the Marquis of Abercorn, for introducing secular and worldly politics into Sunday sermons and for representing the working classes as the subjects of grinding tyranny! He was suspended for a year from his ministry. During this time, Brewster set up soup kitchens to feed local families facing ruin and starvation caused by the recession in the weaving trade.

The Disruption Of the Church of Scotland, in 1843, left many churches without congregations. There was only one man in Paisley who could bring the people flocking back to church and that was Patrick Brewster. He was relieved of his libel and pardoned by the church authorities. Returning in triumph to his post assistant minister at the Abbey, his first sermon was directed to the plight of the poor. That same year he published his famous "Chartist Sermons". For the rest of his life, Brewster continued to work and preach for the rights of the common man.

Patrick Brewster died in 1859. The citizens of Paisley turned out in their thousands to pay their last respects to this champion of the people. In 1863, his statue was erected by public subscription at Woodside Cemetery. This was Paisley's first statue dedicated to a public figure.

Patrick Brewster revolutionised the social and moral behaviour of the first half of the 19th Century. He fought against slavery, bigotry and poverty. He fought for a national system of education. He fought for the cause of temperance. He truly believed that men had the moral right to overthrow tyranny and oppression. As one of the great orators of his time, Brewster's enemies had no answer to his arguments and, for over thirty years, they tried to destroy his reputation and his means of living. However, throughout his life, the people's champion kept faith with his beliefs. Paisley should be proud of him.

Journal versus Herald

Portrait of Richard Watson, owner of the Paisley Herald.

For many years, Paisley readers depended on newspapers published in Edinburgh and Glasgow for their news. There was no local newspaper in Paisley until 1824, when the first copy of the Paisley Advertiser appeared. This was a weekly publication and took a middle line in politics. The Advertiser continued for many years under various editors, among whom was the distinguished poet and author William Motherwell. In 1844, the paper changed its name to the Renfrewshire Advertiser. In 1850, this, Paisley's first newspaper, was merged with the Glasgow Constitutional.

For the next three years, Paisley's news was relegated into the dark corners of Glasgow newspapers. Local people complained that "no town in the British Empire the same size as Paisley, can survive as an independent town, without a local newspaper".

In 1853, the news-deprived people of Paisley got their wish. Not just one, but two new local newspapers appeared on the scene at the same time. A fierce rivalry grew between them and a circulation war broke out in the streets of the town.

The Paisley Journal was first off the mark. The owners of this new newspaper were two local gentlemen, Hay and Waterston, who had for a considerable time made secret preparations to publish a local newspaper. When their prospectus was published on 6th May 1853, the owners declared their intentions. They hoped that their "Paisley Journal would occupy an independent position and pursue an untramelled course in politics and religion." They also added that " while they were attached to the great principles of Protestantism and would support these on all occasions, they would otherwise maintain a position of strict neutrality"!

The first issue of the Paisley Journal appeared on the streets of Paisley on 7th May. A few days after the successful launch of this newspaper, Waterston, one of its owners, noticed a man in Moss Street handing out pamphlets to the Paisley public. Curious to know what the pamphlets contained, he approached the man. On the reading the contents, he discovered to his utter horror that the pamphlet announced that the first edition of another local newspaper, the Paisley Herald, was soon to be published. To add insult to injury, Waterston also read that the owner of the proposed Herald, Richard Watson, was not even a local man and that he claimed to be the first to think up the idea of a new local newspaper! Waterston angrily hurried home down Moss Street, calling the man who had handed out the ominous pamphlet 'a peripatetic quack doctor"!

From his Paisley Journal office in County Place, Waterston vented his anger and frustration at the turn of events by beginning a war of pamphlets against his new rival. He refuted Watson's claim that the Herald had been first in the field and added " The establishment of the Journal had been resolved upon long before I had heard a hint of your intention to favour Paisley with another newspaper. Such being the facts, don't you think. Mr Watson, that it is too much for you to blubber out to the Paisley public, that I have come forward with my newspaper, simply because I was aware of your intentions?"

In a later pamphlet, Watson was again attacked by Waterston. "The projectors of the Paisley Journal have had in contemplation for a considerable time, the starting of a local organ in Paisley. Their arrangements were all but completed when they first heard of the proposal to establish the Herald. Why should we forego a carefully matured plan simply because a stranger to the town had a similar intention?"

Watson was indeed a stranger to the town, but he was first and foremost a gifted, respectable journalist. He took no notice of his rival's grumblings and the Paisley Herald was successfully published on July 9th, only two months after the Paisley Journal. With Watson as its proprietor, the new newspaper was ably written and enjoyed by its readers. It covered articles on politics as well as the social life of the town. Its strongest point, however, was its coverage of municipal and national financial matters. This section of the newspaper appealed greatly to the 'canny' Paisley Buddies.

It was a time when local newspapers were in their hey-day and competition was fierce. Paisley's two rival newspapers held much the same Liberal political views and both were published weekly. For a town the size of Paisley, two such similar newspapers were not commercially viable and the circulation war continued between the rivals.

How much the two opposing factions succeeded in their efforts can be judged by the lives of the respective newspapers. The Paisley Journal ran for only four years, with its last issue rolling off the press on 7th May 1857. The Paisley Herald continued successfully until 1883. Then the printing presses and copyright were sold to James Cook and the newspaper was merged into the Paisley and Renfrewshire Gazette.

PROSPECTUS

OF

THE PAISLEY JOURNAL

And Renfrewshire Gazette.

THAT Paisley, with its large population, industrial interests, and intellectual activity, should possess no Local Newspaper, is subject of inconvenience and regret to the inhabitants, and of surprise to strangers. No town of similar magnitude in the British empire is without its Local Newspaper, while many a far less important place possesses a plurality of Broadsheets. The population of Paisley, within the Parliamentary boundary, is about 48,000, and including those parts of the Abbey Parish which lie beyond the Burgh, it amounts to upwards of 60,000. It is not there alone that the want of a Local Newspaper is felt. Paisley is surrounded by numerous Towns and Villages, of greater or less importance, and more or less connected with it as the centre of the District to which they belong. These places—Renfrew, Pollockshaws, Barrhead, Neilston, Johnstone, Lochwinnoch, Kilbarchan, Bridge of Weir, Houston, &c., and, in fact, the whole Upper Ward of the County of Renfrew, with an aggregate population of 110,000—suffer considerably from the same want. No Newspaper is published in the County, except at Greenock, a distance of sixteen miles from Paisley. That the Upper Ward of Renfrewshire, which teems with Manufactures, should produce no Newspaper, is a most anomalous circumstance. Certain Glasgow Journals devote some degree of attention to Paisley matters; but the limited amount of space which they can afford for the purpose, and the numerous other disadvantages under which they must necessarily labour, in dealing with interests which do not directly concern them, preclude such organs from doing any thing like justice to the locality which they profess to take under their care. It is obvious that the important and multifarious interests of Paisley and its Neighbourhood can never be adequately discussed *in corners of Glasgow Newspapers*. They require an organ of their own to represent them—one specially devoted to the work, and conducted by parties whose primary and paramount duty should be to perform that work efficiently. Such an organ it is now proposed to establish, under the title of **The Paisley Journal and Renfrewshire Gazette**, a Weekly Newspaper, of independent politics and comprehensive general character.

Robert Hay

Robert Hay

Robert Hay 1789-1887.

In 1798, Paisley's weaving trade was brisk. With the prospect of full employment, John Hay, the father of ten children, decided to move to Paisley. Here, the younger sons found employment in weaving, while the daughters were sent to work as finishers on ornamental muslins. One of the youngest members of this family was Robert. He was briefly sent to school, but, as he later recalled, "One by one, members of the family were withdrawn from school and sent to work".

When he was ten, Robert was sent to work the loom. He found this sedentary life dull and tiresome and after reading "Robinson Crusoe", he ran away from home and joined the navy at Greenock. When his distraught father, heard the news, he tried to obtain his son's discharge, "but it could not be obtained without advancing a sum of which, alas he was not master !"

Soon young Hay was serving on various Royal Navy ships, where the "Life was hard and harsh living on the lower decks". On board HMS Culloden, he found the master's mate, Henry Crease, to be a nasty piece of work. Hay recalled that,"He was harsh and tyrannical. From threats he proceeded to blows and not infrequently exercised his skill in the use of a rope's end over my shoulders". However, Culloden's commander, Lieutenant Hawkins, took a kind interest in Hay, who showed great aptitude for improving his education. The commander taught him the rudiments of navigation.

He later served under Rear Admiral Collingwood. Hay wrote of this famous commander, "While we have such men as he, then will the meteor flag grace the mizzen peak, wave protection to commerce, slap defiance to aggressors and flutter in the sunshine of prosperity".

Robert Hay lived an adventurous life at sea for nine years. When he was twenty-two, he returned to Paisley. He had neither seen nor written to his mother, brothers or sisters for many years. Unsure of his welcome, he did not go immediately to his mother's house. He sat in a public house in Causeyside and penned a letter. Robert delivered this letter in person and his mother came to the door. Robert claimed that he was a stranger passing through Paisley and was simply delivering a letter for a friend. His mother eyed him up and down and said, "Ye are him, Sir, ye are him!". Robert replied, "Yes, mother, I am indeed your son." The prodigal had returned.

Advert for Robert Hay and Son Lithographers and engravers 10 High Street, Paisley (1898)

Robert Hay soon got employment in the spring of 1812, working as a steersman on the newly-opened Paisley Canal. After a few days, the expert sailor was promoted to captain on one of the trading boats. Then, in 1813, he was further promoted to canal clerk and storekeeper. This responsible post involved long hours and sometimes troublesome clients. Robert capably dealt with their complaints and efficiently ran his section of the canal.

In 1816, he married a lady "who was the partner of my joys and cares". In his meticulous domestic accounts for that year, he noted that his expenditure was now three times greater than the year before. However, he happily noted in the margin "but gained a wife"!

ADVERTISEMENTS.

ROBERT HAY & SON,

STATIONERS, ACCOUNT-BOOK MAKERS,

Engravers, Lithographers, and General Printers,

10 HIGH STREET, PAISLEY.

Advert for Robert Hay and Son Lithographers and engravers 10 High Street, Paisley (1898)

For many years, Hay worked on canal business. His diary records a typical working day: "Rose at half past four what a valuable hour it is between 5 and 6 in the morning and yet how often does it go to waste! A few small jobs here been lying undone for wont of time. Experienced the inconvenience of wont of attention in pecuniary matters. Forgot that my taxes had been paid last Whit sunday, but I find they have been neglected, which has put me to a few shillings of additional expense".

Hay was always an avid reader. All his spare cash was spent on books and his library contained over 300 volumes. He had great literary aspirations and tried many times to have articles published in a local newspaper. "To appear in print is a small matter and yet I have a considerable penchant in that matter".

In 1828, he finally succeeded. The Paisley Magazine published his articles, entitled "Sam Spritsail", which recalled his early adventures as a sailor. The articles attracted the attention of William Motherwell, who edited that magazine and the newspaper, the Paisley Advertiser. Motherwell thought highly of Hay's literary abilities and good sense and appointed him as sub-editor of the Advertiser in 1830.

When Motherwell left to take up another post, Hay became editor and achieved one of his life's ambitions. He conducted the newspaper with great ability, good taste and moderation. At the same time, Hay acquired a part share in a lithographic and printing business and bought an engraving business belonging to Andrew Blackie. So, the firm of Robert Hay and Sons, lithographers and printers, was founded. The firm gained a reputation as the best in Paisley.

Robert Hay died in 1887. He left two diaries. The first, a chronicle of his life at sea, was published by his grandson in 1953. It was titled "Landsman Hay". The second, covers his life in Paisley (1823-29) and is treasured by the present writer for its vivid accounts of the Paisley scene.

Colinslee Printfield

The designers employed at Colinslee were highly skilled in their juxtaposition of colours. When a printed shawl was viewed from only a short distance, it had all the appearance of the more expensive woven one.

In the early half of the 19th century, next to weaving, block printing was one of the leading industries of Paisley. There were over half a dozen printfields in Paisley, the earliest of which began printing shawls around 1830. These early printed shawls were delicately printed on silk gauzes. Although they were cheaper than the woven varieties, they were still beyond the reach of most families. As the demand for printed shawls increased, so did production at Paisley. The first to enter the field of this lucrative market was the printfield at Blackland Mill. Soon printfields sprang up all over Paisley. Works appeared at Nethercommon, Marshall Lane, Garthland Lane, Lonend, Caledonia Street and Arkleston.

By 1862, such was the success of these companies that the price of a printed Paisley shawl was more affordable and a lady of fashion often owned several printed shawls. It gave her variety in her mode of dress and, being printed on light cotton or silk, the garment was ideal for summer wear. It was much cooler than the heavy woollen woven shawls. The appeal of the printed shawl had an undeniable charm for its wearer.

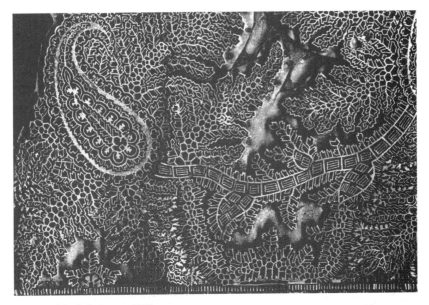

Printing block dating to 1860.
The Paisley Pattern is made up of metal strips pressed into a wooden block.
The technique of how such a delicate printing block was made is now lost.

The largest printfield in the town was at Colinslee in the south end. In its hey-day, over a thousand workers were employed in the factory. Producing Colinslee printed shawls and plaids required a team of designers, block cutters and printers. They were all as highly skilled as their counterparts who produced the woven shawls in other parts of the town. When Paisley shawls reigned supreme, the old weaving town took pride in having two strings to her shawl-making bow.

At Colinslee and at other such similar factories in Paisley, the art of colour printing was to have a profound effect on printed textile design worldwide. Some shawls produced at these Paisley factories show the enormous care in positioning the numerous wooden printing blocks to achieve remarkable colour effects, while others wonderfully mimic the twill of woven shawls. So convincing were the printed shawls that, from a short distance, many could not be distinguished from the woven models. To the lady who could not afford a 'real' Paisley shawl, but wore a printed shawl, this fact was important. The designers employed at Colinslee were so highly skilled in their juxtaposition of colours, that the human eye mixed the colours into a pure, brilliant form. The Paisley designers' subtle technique for shadowed by many years the similar use of colour employed by the French Impressionist painters.

At Colinslee, the design was traced on to blocks of wood, then carved out by the skillful hand of the block cutter. Sometimes as many as twenty printing blocks were required to print one shawl, each with its own colour or pattern. The block printers often worked in sets of four men. Each printer was

These three gentlemen, former Colinslee block printers, achieved considerable local fame. Alexander Brown as a poet, William Brown, his son, as a photographer and Hugh Macdonald as a poet, rambler and author.

responsible for precisely registering his particular colour on the cloth. When the printing block was in contact with the cloth, it was gently hammered down with a lead mallet to make the impression sharp and clear.

One occupation reserved for boys or girls at Colinslee was locally known as a "tearer". The tearer's duty was to spread colour with a brush on to a cloth sieve. The printer then dipped his wooden block into the sieve and applied it to the cloth. The reputation of some of these little 'tearers' was legend in Paisley. They were regarded as "wild country boys" always up to high jinks and their antics were forever being reported in the local press. However, many of the tearers had to behave themselves, as they worked under the stern eye of their fathers, who worked in the factory as respectable block cutters or printers.

These boys kept up their own traditions. On the morning of Hogmanay, the last boy to come in to work was called "Dirty water" and was dipped in the nearby Espedair Burn! Many of these boys rose to eminence in later life. One, indeed, became Lord Mayor of a city in Australia.

Other printworkers also rose to fame. Tom MacEwan, who was a designer at Colinslee, became a well-known artist. Father and son, Alexander and William Brown, who were block printers, achieved local fame as poets and photographers. Hugh Macdonald, the poet, rambler, newspaper editor and author, who is commemorated by the Bonnie Wee Well, was also a block printer at Colinslee.

In 1859, the Colinslee works were finally closed. Some of their beautiful shawls can be seen in Paisley Museum and, no doubt, some still survive tucked away in bottom drawers. William Brown's poem "A Dream of Colinslee" does survive.

"When printing flourished in its golden prime;
When well-curved pines, arranged with graceful fold,
In colours bright, adorned both young and old;
When to possess a printed plaid or shawl
Was still the pride of ladies, one and all".

Alexander Wilson Statue

Alexander Wilson's statue in Abbey Close.
A fitting tribute to one of the world's great naturalists.

Alexander Wilson was born on 6th July 1766, at Seedhill, in an area that had once been within the old walled garden of Paisley Abbey. By a strange quirk of fate, the statue to his memory stands within the present garden wall of the Abbey.

In October 1875, a statue of Alexander Wilson, Paisley's world-famous ornithologist, was unveiled in the grounds of Paisley Abbey. It was an auspicious occasion for the town for, many years after his death, there was at last a fitting memorial to one of her greatest sons.

On the day of the unveiling, the weather was good and the turn out of spectators was large. All classes of people, both rich and poor, had gathered to witness this historic day. Gauze Street and Abbey Close, where the statue stood, were filled with numerous onlookers. A respectable sprinkling of well-dressed ladies added colour to the proceedings. Prominent in the gathering of respectable gentlemen were members of the Alexander Wilson Lodge of Oddfellows dressed in their lodge regalia. It was they who had done so much work to make the splendid statue a reality.

Among the group of distinguished gentlemen present was the sculptor of the monument, John Mossman. When Provost David Murray performed the unveiling ceremony, the seven-foot high bronze statue of Alexander Wilson standing on a ten-foot high polished pedestal of grey granite was displayed to the delighted onlookers. Wilson is depicted leaning against the stump of a tree with his gun propped behind him. At Wilson's feet are his hat and portfolio, on which is resting his pet bird. This little, blue Carolina Parrot went with him on his many wanderings through America. In Wilson's right hand he holds a pencil and in his left a bird he has recently shot and whose plumage he is evidently studying.

As a work of art and as a memorial to Wilson, the statue was a remarkable piece of work. From all accounts, the sculptor had even managed to capture Wilson's likeness by studying earlier portraits and engravings of the great man, notably the portrait by James Craw.

Alexander Wilson had died in 1813. In America he was a famous man, but in his birthplace of Paisley no monument had ever been erected in his honour. This was partly put to rights as late as 1841, when a memorial tablet was placed in the wall of the house at Seedhill where he had been born. The Alexander Wilson Lodge of Oddfellows had taken a prominent part in this small, but, to them, important affair. After all, their lodge was named after the great man himself. But, to the Oddfellows, this small tribute was never enough. They wished a more fitting memorial to be erected in Wilson's home town.

The Oddfellows formed a monument committee, which first met in 1844 in the Railway Arms Inn. Not wishing to confine their activities to lodge members only, outsiders were brought in. One of these was Thomas Crichton, who had been an intimate friend of Wilson's and his first biographer. However, despite a larger committee which included other local gentlemen of standing, funds for a monument were slow to come in.

Then in 1855, George Ord of Philadelphia, who was one of Wilson's earliest and most intimate friends in America, came to Paisley on a pilgrimage to see Wilson's birthplace at Seedhill. While he was in Paisley, George Ord heard that funds were being gathered for amonument to Wilson. Ord promised to help. When he returned to America, he gathered substantial funds from influential friends and institutions. The main contributor was The Academy of Natural Sciences of Philadelphia, whose members held Wilson's great book, "The American Ornithology" in high esteem.

Four years later, the monument committee had, at last, collected enough funds to commission a statue of Wilson.

In 1862, the committee invited leading sculptors from London, Edinburgh and Glasgow to submit designs for the proposed statue for their approval. Glasgow's leading sculptor, John Mossman, won the competition.

The selection of a suitable site was next on the committee's agenda. For many years, they had anxiously looked about Paisley. When a corner of the grounds of Paisley Abbey became available due to the demolition of some old houses, the long wait for an appropriate site was over.

As Provost Murray unveiled the statue he said, "I trust this statue will not only commemorate the memory of the great man as it is meant to do, but that it will be a beacon in after ages, to point the youths of Paisley to what one townsman has done. I accept the statue on behalf of the town. It will be a pride and pleasure to Paisley in all future times to possess and conserve this monument".

Alexander Wilson was born on 6th July 1766, at Seedhill, in an area that had once been within the old walled garden of Paisley Abbey. By a strange quirk of fate, the statue to his memory stands within the present garden wall of the Abbey.

David Murray

David Murray (1807-1876), who served three terms as Provost of Paisley, and who did not spare himself in the service of his town.

David Murray was born in 1807 at 24 Smithhills, Paisley. His father, William, ran a prosperous painter-decorators shop in Gilmour Street. David's family were well-connected. His maternal grandparents, the Wilsons, were related to David Dale of New Lanark fame. It was these two who had such a deep influence on the bringing up of their grandson. As his grandparent's house was situated next door, on most evenings David sat with them around the large ingle-neuk fireplace, where he was told wonderful stories about Scottish history. By the light of an oil lamp, his grandfather would then solemnly read aloud from the family Bible.

David was brought up in Paisley at a time when the town was full of soldiers. The country was waging a war with Napoleon on the continent. Young David often saw crowds of his townspeople rushing to meet the mail coach. As the distant sound of the guard's horn was heard and the flash of his red coat was sighted, every eye became fixed on the guard's flag. If the coach brought news of a great victory, the flag would be waved triumphantly and flaunted in front of the cheering crowd.

In 1819, David left school to become apprenticed to a local medical practitioner, Robert McKechnie M.D. The doctor thought highly of his new apprentice and found him to be most obliging, earnest, studious and of a quiet disposition. David absorbed as much learning as he could from medical text books and developed a great love of chemistry. However, an experiment he was conducting went badly wrong and exploded in his face, leaving him scarred for life.

Then David's father died and, to support the family, he had to leave his medical studies and take up the helm of the family business. David was quite happy to comply, as witnessing the crude surgery of those days had put him off medicine for life. Painting and decorating houses in Paisley was less traumatic!

It was during Provost Murray's reign that many street improvements were made in Paisley. One such was just after 1876, when all the old buildings on the North side of the High Street were swept away.

In 1824, to further his education, David joined a set of young gentlemen who had formed the "Junior Literary Society" in Paisley. The members presented papers on topical subjects ranging from religion to politics, then debates followed. David, who was of Moderate Liberal persuasion, presented a paper on Parliamentary reform. Significantly, his paper was an uncanny prediction of things to come, years before the great Reform Act came into being.

The year before the Reform Act was finally passed in 1832, David Murray made a celebrated speech advocating the radical reforms it proposed. He stood on a gravestone in the old Low Church in New Street and addressed the crowd. His Paisley audience acclaimed him as a rising politician. In 1836 when he was only 29, Murray's aptitude for politics gained him a place in the town council. A year later, he became Burgh Treasurer and, in 1840, a senior Baillie.

At this time, Paisley suffered her worst-ever trade depression. Some 15,000 weavers were out of work and many families were at near-starvation level. Only soup kitchens and public relief kept them alive. During this miserable time, Baillie David Murray emerged as a leader of his poor, wretched towns people. In the harsh, winter months of 1841, Murray spent many weeks in London, urging Sir Robert Peel's government to answer the cries for help from the starving community of Paisley. Eventually, the government answered his pleas and some aid was sent to Paisley.

A relief committee was set up in the town with Murray acting as chairman. As well as the government aid, amounts, large and small, were donated from around the country. £53,000 was distributed over a two-year period to feed the poor of Paisley. However, there never seemed to be enough money to go round and Murray recalled his despair at the time. "Many a morning during these dreary months I rose from my bed fully realising I knew of no means to keep the starving population in existence".

When the worst of the crisis was over, Paisley showed its gratitude to Murray by electing him provost three times, in 1844, in 1847 and, again, in 1869. Murray's townsmen knew that they could turn to him "to do the town some service" and that he was the man in town who could "ca' the gir", (turn the wheels). This he did.

In 1871, he began measures to remove the shadow of bankruptcy from the town. A typical example was the purchasing of the town's gasworks from its private owners, thus making gas cheaper for the people. Murray also busied himself with badly-needed street improvements, notably in laying out a new St Mirin Street to smarten up the town and improve trade.

As provost, Murray had to go to London to present his Improvement Bill to Parliament. In London he met an exiled Paisley lady. She told Provost Murray that she had recently visited her home town and wondered why he was so hot and bothered about improving "sic a place as Paisley". She ended by saying," The only way to improve Paisley is tae ding it doon! "Fortunately, the provost did not agree!

Murray's reputation for getting things done soon spread throughout Scotland and he was given the accolade "Provost of Scotland."David Murray was truly one of the great provosts of Paisley. From the painter who whistled as he decorated a room, to the provost who roared like a lion was a very long step. So long indeed that few painters' ladders ever reached such heights!

John Smart

Portrait of John Smart, Headmaster of the John Neilson Institution 1859-1862.

In 1853, a young man climbed up the steep slope at Oakshaw Brae to take up a new teaching appointment. His destination was the John Neilson Institution. The school, with its elegant dome, was but one year old. The new teacher had been appointed as master in Classics and Mathematics, a strange combination nowadays, but not so in Victorian times.

View of the old school affectionately known in Paisley as 'The parritch bowl'.

John Smart, the new teacher, arrived in Paisley as a young man of twenty-four. He was born in 1829, in the parish of Larbert. His father had a humble occupation in the Carron Ironworks and young John's story was a familiar one. He had been a lad o' pairts, triumphing over poor health and poverty with talent and true grit. A self-taught man with unlimited zeal and an analytical mind, he made teaching his calling.

Settling in to the Neilson School, he soon brought about a fresh approach to his chosen subjects. In his classroom, Smart, a man of singular ability, became a teacher of no ordinary stamp. This tall, thin man with remarkably brilliant eyes exhibited a perfect control over his classroom. He rarely achieved this control 'by the might of the rod'. Nor did he employ the use of punishment exercises, known in Paisley as 'task lessons'. His control was achieved by the kindness which he extended to all his pupils. Unusually for that time, Smart believed that corporal punishment degraded both master and pupil. Such was his command that, to discipline his pupils, all he needed to do was give a stern warning or sometimes stamp his feet loudly on the classroom floor! If pupils became restless or inattentive, he would order them to "Stand.... right about face..... resume your seat!"

Smart brought his vast store of knowledge to every subject he taught. His teaching was avant garde for its time. He pioneered the use of teaching aids in the classroom to add interest and he had the gift of making pupils think that they had in no small way contributed to the lessons. Rows of children could be seen 'with a look of satisfaction on their faces' at the end of a lesson.

Smart's concern for his pupils was not confined to the classroom. If he noticed a pupil poring over a book at playtime, he would, in a kindly tone, tell the pupil to go and play, as a time was coming when "there would be plenty of work and no play". Smart often joined his pupils in the playground to play a friendly game of shinty. This was almost unheard of in a strict Victorian Paisley!

Smart's teaching department received high praise from all quarters. In 1855, a government inspector reported that "the Latin pupils are unusually well-grounded". Another report stated "that the numbers taking Classics had increased under Mr Smart. This is proof at once of his skill as a teacher and of the progress of this institution as a centre of education".

Smart's dedication to his pupils did not go unnoticed. In 1859, in recognition of his services, the school trustees appointed him headmaster. Under Smart's rule, the J.N.I. became one of the most highly-respected schools in the West of Scotland. Some of Smart's 'old boys' were now lifting prizes at Glasgow University and going on to glittering careers.

In Paisley, Smart had gained quite a reputation in religious matters. He believed in freedom of thought and was by no means satisfied with the opinions of the orthodox theology of his day. In a series of lectures given in Paisley, he expressed his strong dissent against these commonly held opinions. He also appeared in public debates in which he defended some aspects of the Christian faith against a group of people called the "Secularists". In 1861, he published a small volume which he called "The New Theology". In this work, Smart set out his independent religious views. The book caused a small sensation in Paisley. There was tongue-wagging and shaking of heads, but no hunt for heresy.

Paisley was stunned to hear of his death in 1862. John Smart died at the early age of 33, 'burnt out' with overwork. His health had never been robust and, in his last year as headmaster, it was noticed how pale he had become. It was said, "he had the look of one who burned the midnight oil too much or was working beyond his strength".

J.J.Lamb

Portrait of architect James Jamieson Lamb, who typified the new breed of Victorian professional gentlemen.... well educated with wide interests.

James Jamieson Lamb was born in Paisley on 24th October,1817. His father, James Lamb, was a well-known architect and land surveyor in Paisley. Young James was brought up at Underwood Cottage, which his father had designed and built in 1824. James was educated in the best "higher and aristocratic", schools that Paisley had to offer. He was placed, firstly, at the Burgh English school, then at the Commercial School and, finally, at Paisley Grammar School, where, under the watchful eye of the rector, John Peddie, young James won two prizes for Latin and one for "Superiority in drawing".

When James left school, his father took him into his own practice to train as an architect and land surveyor. Young James was following the family tradition, as his grandfather, too, had been a busy architect in Paisley. When his father died in 1843, James took over the family business and, over the years, extended the practice, both in Paisley and Renfrewshire. One of his largest commissions was to design the School of Design in Gilmour Street. This large building, with its symmetrical facade, was opened in 1848, to educate the artisan designers of the town in art and science.

At an early age, James developed a taste for fine books and, over the years, collected a large and valuable library. This was particularly rich in local literature, on which he became an authority. He would spent hours adding his own notes about local authors on the fly-leaves of their respective books.

His profession as an architect gave him an interest in visiting and studying old cathedrals and abbeys. Another antiquarian interest which James held dear, was collecting coins. He amassed a huge cabinet full of old and ancient coins. His most cherished piece was the very rare "Crookston Dollar". It was beyond value in his eyes.

Autograph hunters are nothing new. Throughout his life, James Lamb collected autographs and letters of famous statesmen, military heroes, poets, celebrated authors and actors. So large was the collection, that it took fifteen large folio volumes to gather them together! These can now be seen in the Paisley Reference Library.

Lamb's design for the Grammar School and Academy built at Oakshaw in 1863. A few years ago, this, the last major example of his work in Paisley, was left to become derelict and was burnt down.

James also loved poetry and, indeed, wrote some fine verses himself. His poem, "Winter Stanzas", is an example,

"But still the monotonous rain drops fall,
Drip, drip, from the clammy eaves;
The ivy has lost its hold on the wall,
The daisy is dead, and rotting lies,
Nature is sick of the cheerless skies,
And man will fall like the leaves."

James Lamb was a fervent admirer of drama, particularly Shakespearian drama. He always attended performances by any celebrated actor who visited Paisley. He thought this an "exquisite treat". So fond was he of Shakespeare, that, in 1872, he offered a prize to the member of the Paisley Horticultural Society who could best display 'Shakespearian' flowers and quotations.

To help educate the 'working classes' of Paisley, James Lamb gave a series of very successful Sunday evening lectures to the Artisans' Institute. He was one of the chief promoters of this institute and took a warm interest in it, from its early beginnings in 1847.

The literary pursuits of James Lamb were varied. His versatile pen furnished articles for daily, weekly and monthly publications. His column in the Paisley Herald, "Talk across the Walnuts and the Wine", told the current gossip of the day. These articles became so popular with his Paisley readership, that they were read before any other part of the paper! He contributed to Ogilvie's famous "Imperial Dictionary", in 1853 and to the "Harp of Renfrewshire", in 1871.

Memorandum note by Lamb to one of his clients, dated 1877.

As a public figure in Paisley, civic honours came his way. In 1857, he was made a commissioner of the peace for the county and elected a Paisley Town Councillor the same year. Two years later, he became a baillie of the burgh. In these capacities, he discharged his civic and criminal duties "honestly and fearlessly, tempering his judgments with justice and mercy".

James Lamb was the first President of the Tannahill Club when it was founded in 1858. The club was formed to commemorate the anniversaries of the poet's birthday. Throughout his life, James Lamb had been a great admirer of Robert Tannahill, just like his father, who had known and befriended the poet. Presiding at a meeting of the Tannahill Club, he said, " We are specially proud of our Paisley lyricist, this gentle poet of ours, Robert Tannahill".

In his later years, he wrote a memoir of Tannahill to include in an edition of the poet's songs and poems. He dedicated the work to the members of the Tannahill Club. It was published after his death.

James Lamb died on 27th September, 1872, leaving a widow and eight children. He had been an affectionate husband and a kind parent. Beloved by a large circle of friends, his sudden death caused a general despondency in the town. After a large, public funeral, he was buried in Woodside Cemetery.

His major public buildings in Paisley, the School of Design in Gilmour Street and the Grammar School and Academy at Oakshaw, have, over the years, sadly disappeared. So, Paisley has lost these fine examples of the work of this distinguished local architect.

The Brodie Park

Brodie Park Avenue appears in the background. The old timber greenhouse can be clearly seen. The foreground shows the Dooslan Stane, the four 'elephant's feet' and the cast iron canopy over the drinking fountain.

Nestling in a leafy enclave of Paisley's South End is the Brodie Park. This spacious tree-lined area, surrounded by suburban villas and flats, was the gift to the town by a respected banker, Robert Brodie.

Robert Brodie was born in Kerse Farm in Lochwinnoch Parish on 3rd June, 1807. The farm was owned in turn by his father and grandfather. The young Robert was educated in the parish schools of Kilbirnie and Beith and, at the age of 15, began his working life in Johnstone as an invoice clerk with Houston & Co. With his aptitude for book-keeping, he soon attracted the attention of his employer, Mr Houston the Laird of Johnstone, who, at that time, was a director of the Paisley Union Bank. In 1823, he appointed Brodie a junior clerk in his bank. This employment brought the young man to work in its Paisley branch the following year.

Over his years working in several banks, Brodie rose from clerk, to accountant and finally manager of the National Bank in Paisley. He was to remain in service with this bank until 1870, when failing health forced him to resign.

Robert Brodie led a singularly quiet, unobtrusive life. He never married. He had, however, one driving ambition in life, to save enough money to buy back the family farm in Lochwinnoch. Brodie's father, through an unfortunate legal wrangle, had lost the ownership of the family farm. Over the years, Brodie

The Carriagehill entrance to the park (C 1906). To the left is the park keeper's house. The roof of the old bandstand appears in the background, together with Rowat's house, St. Margaret's.

had managed to make a small fortune, not through wild speculation, but by investing his money judiciously as only a capital banker could do. He excelled in banking matters, was well-read, well-educated and a fine accountant. However, when he had finally made enough money to buy back the family farm, the owners refused to sell it and Brodie was unable to fulfill his life's ambition.

Instead, he bought a large estate in his adopted town of Paisley, where he was a much respected figure. This estate lay in the South End of Paisley and formed part of the old lands of Carriagehill. His mansion, called Carriagehill House, with its well laid-out gardens, stood on Carriagehill (now Braids Road) on land which is now a children's playground. Brodie stayed there happily for the last fifteen years of his life.

Such was Brodie's love of Paisley, that, in 1870 the year before his death, he made a will conveying the grounds of Carriagehill to the Burgh of Paisley. He stipulated that twenty-two acres of his estate were to be used as "pleasure grounds and places of public recreation for the inhabitants of Paisley".

The Brodie Park was formally opened in 1877 by his old friend Provost Murray, in the company of ten thousand cheering spectators. Specimen trees were planted around the perimeter of the new park and wide carriageways cut through it. It was then the custom for rich Paisley families to ride through the

Looking up the park from Carriagehill. The park keeper's house and ladies' waiting room appears on the left. The roof of the old bandstand appears in the background.

park in horse and carriage displaying their finery. At the Mary Street entrance, ladies could could rest and shelter in the specially-built Ladies' waiting-room adjoining the park-keeper's house. The park was adorned with benches, formal flower beds, shrubs and drinking fountains.

Great excitement took place in the park with the arrival of two kangaroos. The animals had been presented to the town in February 1885, by the Marquis of Bute. A small house was built to accommodate the animals but, sadly, they died within a month of their arrival. Paisley's winter climate must have been too much for them!

In 1896, a splendid octagonal bandstand with a 'witch's hat' roof was built at the top of the park, to the design of local architect W. D. McLennan. Funds raised from the famous Tannahill Glen Concerts paid for its erection. It was from this time on that music in the 'Brodie' during the summer months proved to be "largely appreciated by all classes of the community". Bands and concert parties played on Sundays.

Music of a different order took place in the park some years later. In 1908, Harry Lauder appeared with Dame Nelly Melba. The world-famous entertainers played gramophone records from the bandstand to a spellbound Paisley audience.

Another arrival in the park came in the shape of of a shiny boulder. In 1896, Paisley's own 'wee magic stone,' the Dooslan Stane, was prised from its original setting in Rowan Street and rolled to rest in the park. It sits squatly between four plinth stones removed from Paisley's old Tolbooth. These four old stones are known locally as the "the elephant's feet" and have been climbed upon by generations of Paisley children. Another old date stone, inscribed 1757 and also taken from the old Tolbooth, now lies unseen beneath a circular walled shrub bed at the park entrance.

Every year, the revived Sma Shot Parade gathers round the Dooslan Stane before making its way in to the town.

Today, the Brodie is still a popular park. It is a place to walk the dog, play pitch and putt and admire the flower beds. The Ladies' waiting-room, with its wooden window seats, and the parkie's house are now being restored. Gone is the fine Victorian bandstand, the fine wrought iron gates and railings, the greenhouse and the cast-iron fountains. Gone too is the wee shelter at the top of the park where many a courting couple was disturbed by the local policeman doing his evening rounds!

St. Margaret's

View of St Margaret's, the home of the Rowat Family.

Overlooking Brodie Park stands a large mansion house called St Margaret's. It was originally built in 1879 for a well-known Paisley shawl manufacturer, William Rowat, who at that time lived in nearby Rosehill Cottage. When his business prospered, he commissioned the architect John Hutchison, who was a near neighbour, to design a large, stone-built, Scots Baronial mansion house.

Specimen trees were planted around the garden perimeter and curved carriageways led to an imposing front entrance. At the rear, garden walkways skirted around terraced lawns. The new garden reflected William Rowat's deep love of nature. He was particularly proud of his flower garden and two large greenhouses full of exotic plants.

William Rowat and his two brothers, Robert and Thomas, had inherited a successful shawl manufacturing business in Paisley from their father Robert, who had a considerable trade in "thibet" shawls.

William Rowat, besides being a shawl manufacturer, had other business concerns. He was a director in the Doloi Tea Company and held an interest in Rowat's Pickles.

Jessie Rowat (1864-1948)

Other members of his family were Claud Rowat, a Glasgow stockbroker, and Alexander Rowat, who owned a Glasgow wire working business.

The substantially built and finely detailed stonework of their new home, St Margaret's reflected the wealth and good taste and, indeed, the high social standing the Rowats held in Paisley. The family were often honoured guests at social events in Paisley, such as the grand "Evening Conversatione" at the inauguration of the Town Hall in 1882.

Jessie Rowat, one of William's three daughters, was brought up at St Margaret's. Her father, in a view radical for the times, insisted that all his daughters receive a proper education. Jessie more than fulfiled his wishes. She studied at Glasgow School of Art and it was there that she met and married, in 1889, its Principal, Fra Newbury. She became an artist in her own right and established an embroidery department at the art school which brought her international recognition. Jessie and her husband were involved in choosing the design for Glasgow's new art school. It was by her husband's star pupil and protege, Charles Rennie Mackintosh. It is interesting to note that Mackintosh was first apprenticed to John Hutchison, the designer of her father's house in Paisley.

As well as owning St Margaret's in Paisley, the Rowats had a town house in Glasgow at Kingsborough Gardens. In 1901, they commissioned Mackintosh to redesign the interior. So it is highly likely that the, now, world-famous architect may have visited St Margaret's to consult his Paisley clients and friends. Hearsay has it that Charles and Margaret Mackintosh attended the wedding of Claud Rowat and Miss Veitch of Friarshall, at Paisley Abbey.

John Hutchison, the architect of St. Margaret's (1841-1908).

When William Rowat returned home each day, he was met by a gathering of local children in Brodie Park. They knew full well that he would distribute the sweets he had bought for them. Even his household staff were given nine sweets a week each, but only on pay day!

Of a generous nature, William purchased a piece of ground at the junction of Park Road and Stanely Road which he donated to the town. This is still kept as a rose garden. He also gifted to the town his valuable library, which contained much local material and works on Robert Burns. It is now known as the "Rowat Collection".

When William Rowat returned home each day , he was met by a crowd of children in Brodie Park. They knew full well that he would distribute the sweets he had bought for them.

In politics, William Rowat was a staunch Liberal He spent most of his mornings in the smoking room of the Liberal Club, where he had the honour of meeting Prime Minister Asquith.

In 1920, Rowat died in his 90th year. One of his daughters, who had cared for her father, was the only occupant left in St Margaret's and, shortly after this, the house was sold to W.Y. Fleming of Fleming and Ferguson, shipbuilders. In 1928, the house became the property of the local parish council and was converted to an old people's home. The old folks who stayed there, then, were expected to take their turn at polishing the plethora of brass work in the house or in cleaning the many fireplaces! In 1978, the hospital celebrated its Golden Jubilee. By this time, the house exterior had become cluttered with ramps, unsightly fire escapes and outbuildings.

The building ceased to be a hospital and, left unoccupied, became more and more dilapidated. In this state, it had a moment of fame when it was used as a backdrop in an episode of "Taggart".

However, William Rowat, its original proud owner would be pleased to see his house today. It has been tastefully restored to its original condition by a firm of local builders and is now, once more, one of Paisley's finest flatted mansion houses.

James Whitelaw Craig

Portrait of J.W. Craig (1849-1880), one of Paisley's remarkable naturalists.

Paisley Museum is rich in its wonderful collections of natural history specimens. Thousands of birds, butterflies and beetles forming sizeable collections have been donated over the years, mainly by local naturalists. Until the the late 1950's, the Natural History gallery had wall-to wall glass cases, which brimmed over with all kinds of specimens.

Readers may remember one collection on display which was quite outstanding. It was neatly labelled "The Craig Collection of Australian Natural History". It was a collection of birds, animals, insects, butterflies, moths and beetles and it also included such curiosities as Aboriginal spears, clubs and boomerangs.

The naturalist who had gathered together this unique collection was a local man, James Whitelaw Craig. James was born in March 1849 in a suburban villa in Gateside, then an unspoilt country area of Paisley (now Renfrew Road). The Craig family had moved there to allow their father, Archibald, to be near his engineering works at the Vulcan Foundry .

As the son of a prosperous engineer, James was sent to finish his education at a private boarding school, Montgreenan near Kilwinning. After leaving school with an excellent education, James began an apprenticeship in his father's engineering firm, Craig and Fullerton. However, James' weak health was most unsuited to the confines of an engineering factory. Throughout his youth, his health had never been robust and James rarely took part in sporting

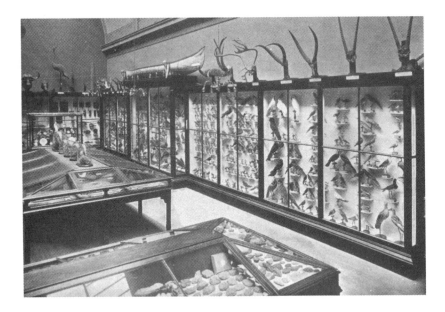

Craig's collection behind glass as it appeared in Paisley Museum in 1908.

activities like his friends. He preferred to spend his spare time in quiet study reading his favourite authors. Natural History books were of particular interest to him, as well as the history books of his native town.

In the autumn of 1873, much to the consternation of his family and friends, James' health declined. History has not handed down the nature of his affliction, but he may well have been suffering from that dreaded scourge of the Victorian age, consumption. James was ordered by his doctor to spend the rest of the winter in the warm south- west of France, at the health resort of Pau.

James Craig's stay in France improved his health a little. He now had time and energy to study his favourite subject, Natural History. He made numerous field trips around Pau, Biarritz and Bordeaux, collecting specimens of birds, insects and plants, all of which he neatly catalogued in his meticulously-kept daily diary. For January 9th, 1874 he records, "Beautiful day, but cold in the shade. Spend most of the day skinning birds, mounting plants etc...."Ever watchful of his health, James wrote, "Got weighed today and found myself the same as I was a month ago".

James returned to Paisley in August 1874, but, once again, he was advised by his doctor to go to another warm climate, Australia. He sailed from Greenock at the end of August and arrived in Melbourne six weeks later. James found the unique flora and fauna of this large continent a delight. He made many field trips to the country around Melbourne, Sydney and Brisbane, gathering a huge amount of specimens for his Natural History collection.

In Australia, James shot kangaroos, wallabies and snakes, all in the name of science.

It was a marvel that a young man in such a weak state of health could gather such a large and varied an amount of material in the space of only two years. Not only did he shoot all the birds and animals, but he also skinned and preserved them with his own hands. Not only did he capture all the butterflies and other insects, but he arranged them into display cases himself. This wholesale killing of animals as specimens was the accepted practice in Victorian times. In Australia, James shot kangaroos, wallabies and snakes, all in the name of science. By June 1896, his diary recorded that he had now collected 808 birds!

He made friends with the Aboriginal people, bought curiosities from them, studied their habits and language and even compiled some of their vocabulary in his journal. James' daily schedule was hectic. It was as if he knew he had little time left. His health forced him to return to Paisley. Despite another few months in the warm climate of Pau, his health never improved. James died in September 1880, aged only 32, at the family home in Paisley.

It was only after his death that a manuscript dealing with the history of Paisley had been found among his papers. This was published privately in 1881, with the title "Historical Notes on Paisley and its Neighbourhood".

Twenty-eight years after his death, the meticulously-kept journals of his natural history trips were discovered. These were published privately in 1908, under the title "Diary of a Naturalist".

Craig 's natural history collection is still held in Paisley Museum, although it is not all on show. The collection is quite remarkable for its size, varied contents and for the short period during which it was amassed. James Whitelaw Craig was 'naturally' a remarkable Paisley Buddie.

Peter Brough

In 1897, Princess Louise laid the foundation stone of Paisley Technical School.

When Peter Brough died in Paisley in 1883, the popular conception of the man was that, "He was a kind of miserly old bachelor", who had been a draper in the High Street and had died leaving "an awfu' lot of money". Paisley people could only remember him as an old man dressed in unfashionable, sometimes worn clothing. In his latter years, his recluse-like habits, combined with his well-known thrift and frugality, served to deepen the impression that Peter Brough was a miserly man.

However, Brough was certainly no miser, but a man who became one of Paisley's greatest benefactors. He was to bequeath his large fortune to many worthy causes in the town of his adoption. Today, his numerous legacies still flow through Paisley.

In 1816, Peter Brough, aged nineteen, arrived in Paisley to take charge of a newly- opened draper's shop. The owner, a Mr Harvey, soon found his Paisley shop was unprofitable and offered to sell the stock to a somewhat reluctant young Peter. However, Peter agreed to take over. He borrowed £20 from his father and, within two years, had improved the   business so much that he bought a double-fronted shop at 96 High Street. The business continued to prosper and, four years later, he set up his elder   brother, David, in another draper's shop near Paisley Cross. This shop was the first in the town to be illuminated by the newly-fashionable gas lighting and caused a sensation among the burghers of Paisley! It was typical of Peter's innovative flair in business matters.

The Brough residence for nurses at Oakshaw was opened officially in 1897 by Princess Louise.

In 1820, his father's business as a grain dealer in Old Scone, where Peter was born, went bankrupt. Peter nobly paid all the creditors in full. This was hardly the action of a man thought by some to be a miser. As Paisley people would say, he was just 'careful'.

With his canny business acumen, Peter grew ambitious and, by 1826, owned six shops, three of them in Paisley. The shops became the talk of the town, because shopping at Brough's was much cheaper than anywhere else.

With his business now prosperous and secure, Peter turned his attention to local politics. In 1830, he entered the Town Council, becoming a bailie two years later. As a Liberal, he supported the New Burgh Reform Bill of 1833, which he regarded as a "great healing measure, calculated to strengthen and establish various institutions".

Peter Brough took up many positions for the good of the town. He became a Justice of the Peace, a director of the Paisley Water Company, Chairman of the Paisley Security Savings Bank and president of the Draper's Association. In the latter post, he "exercised a healthy influence among those who followed his favourite occupation". There was no end to to his many talents. Indeed, so much of his time was taken up with public affairs that he took in a partner to help run the business.

Peter Brough was now in the prime of his life. With his immense energy and first class business abilities, he was earning £1500 a year, a vast sum for those days. He could afford to stay in a large mansion in Oakshaw. As a man of substance, he had his portrait painted.

His business partner, James Sharp, has left us with a graphic account of Brough's appearance. "He was in stature rather above the average, being five feet ten inches in height and somewhat slender in person. His complexion was pale, but his features good. With a well-formed mouth, prominent nose, bright sparkling eyes and high and well-developed forehead. He cultivated no beard or moustache and, having become prematurely bald from early manhood, he wore a wig. He dressed carefully and well, being usually attired in navy blue frock coat, black vest and trousers. No one ever saw him in a suit of tweeds. He was scrupulously clean in his linen, the marked peculiarity of which was the extreme height of his shirt collar, which covered the full half of his cheek and was as stiffly starched as Beau Brummel's".

His spare time was now taken up with the investment of his money in shares. Yet Peter Brough still lived the frugal life. Once, when taking a train to the coast, he was asked by his gardener, "Shall I take out first-class tickets?" "No Sandie" was the reply, "A third-class ticket will take us as quickly to Gourock as a first!"

But, ironically, it was through sound investment in railways that Peter Brough increased his fortunes. It was a Paisley man, Sir James Watson, a founder member of the Glasgow stock exchange and later Lord Provost of that city, who advised Brough in his financial dealings, some of which involved sums of up to £70,000!

When Peter Brough died on 18th July 1883, he left a fortune upwards of £155,000.

No one in Paisley realised just how much the man was worth until his will was published. People were amazed when they saw the bequests the one-time draper had left for the good of the town.

Among his many bequests was one that his house in Oakshaw be given as a home for nurses. (fondly remembered in Paisley as the Brough Nurses) Money was given over to such establishments as the Paisley Ragged and Industrial School, the John Neilson Institution and the National Bible Society. Money was given to his own Free High Church, to build The Margaret Brough Hall in memory of his sister. Funds were left to provide coals for the poor of Paisley and to deserving widows in the town. Paisley Infirmary also received a large bequest.

Perhaps most importantly for the future of Paisley was the distribution of the balance of his estate by his trustees. An annual sum of £300 was to be used to establish a science lectureship in the Burgh of Paisley. The remainder helped set up a much needed Technical School. This was the founding of what is now The University of Paisley.

Peter Brough is buried in Woodside Cemetery. His granite tombstone aptly bears the inscription "He lived not for himself, but for others".

Hugh Kilpatrick

*Oil Portrait of Hugh Kilpatrick, best known in Paisley
as the poet with the ready pen, 'Eagle Eye'.*

Hugh Kilpatrick was born at Smith Street, Charleston on 23rd November 1823. His father and grandfather were both weavers in the town who held radical political views far in advance of their time. His grandfather's sister was the famous "Radical Nan", one of the few female leaders in Paisley advocating political and social reform. Hugh's grandfather, William, had also been a ringleader of the Radicals in Paisley. He had been pressed-ganged into the Royal Navy during the American War of Independence and served there until the end of the war. When he was released from the navy, William returned from America to work his loom in Paisley. He became a preacher among the Baptists of Paisley and, during his ministrations, had the honour of baptising David Dale of New Lanark Mill fame.

Kilpatrick sent one of his poems to his hero Garibaldi and much to the poet's delight, received a favourable reply!

Like his grandfather, young Hugh was apprenticed to the loom. During his training he was initiated not only to the craft of weaving, but to his family's strong political views. These radical views Hugh was to hold until his death.

Hugh was ambitious and enterprising and, early in life, set up a business as a manufacturer or 'cork' in the town of Paisley. At this time, unfortunately for Hugh, the shawl trade was in a temporary decline. Many of the town's shawl makers had come to grief and Hugh was no exception. He became bankrupt. Like many Paisley men, he was forced to emigrate and, in 1862, he sailed to the United States of America. In America he prospered briefly in business and returned to Paisley seven years later. With the money he had saved abroad he managed to pay off all his debtors in Paisley.

With his remaining funds, Hugh managed to set up a business in Orchard Street. He later moved to Moss Street, but around the early 1890s, he failed in business for the second time. To sustain himself, he became a collector of accounts for various business men. From this he made an adequate, if precarious, livelihood.

Throughout his life, Hugh Kilpatrick had written verses in the true spirit of the Paisley poets. However, only those written when he reached the age of fifty have survived. At this time of his life, he began to record local and national events through his prose and verse and he gained quite a reputation in his home town under his self-styled pen name "Eagle Eye".

One of the highlights of his life occurred when he sent one of his poems to General Garibaldi, the famous Italian patriot. The poem was especially written in 1872 to console the general on the loss of his daughter. Garibaldi was so touched by the words that he wrote in reply praising Kilpatrick for his "beautiful poetry".

Provost Cochran was the 'victim' of one of Kilpatrick's poems.

108

Poetry, perhaps less "beautiful" but nevertheless heartfelt, was written on the death of his faithful dog. Kilpatrick wrote:

"My wee bit dugie's noo nae mair,
An', oh! I rue his absence sair,
He aye was ready, keen tae share
His joy wi' ony".

Throughout his life, Kilpatrick found pleasure in music and on many a social occasion played his violin to his friends.

"When I thy lovely neck caress,
It's varnish pure and thin
And firm the strings my fingers press
Thine answering tones thy love confess
O, charming violin".

During the times when he was hard pressed to provide for his family or when his wife wanted cash for clothes or shoes, Kilpatrick freely admitted all he could do was hand her strips of poetry. He thought of himself as "a hardened, worthless wretch. "However, he still kept his sense of humour and, during his long life, he wrote many letters to the local press poking fun at the financially successful people of Paisley. One of his poems was aimed at Paisley's ruling citizens. Provost Cochran better known by the sobriquet of "Wee Clearheid" was one of his targets,

"There's wee Clearheid, for forty years
The body's done his best;
An' what I gie him credit for,
He's feather'd his ain nest.
He's been a politician bright,
Champion o' working class;
An mony a snap and sneer he's got
An been in mony a mess".

Hugh Kilpatrick died in 1909, aged 86. His friends arranged to have a book of his poems published and the proceeds given to the poet's aged widow.

Mrs Jane Arthur

Portrait of Mrs Jane Arthur of Barshaw, one of Paisley's benefactors.

Mrs Jane Arthur was known in Paisley as "The Lady Bountiful of Barshaw". As Jane Glen, she had married James Arthur, a rich, wholesale draper in 1847. They purchased Barshaw House and estate in 1858. That year, the house was described as "a beautiful little estate and mansion house" and "there is no more hospitable mansion than Barshaw". Jane Arthur, it appears, "was in place at Barshaw doing the many duties of a wife, in a pleasant, frank, genial way which made the household happy".

However, on one occasion, she was not a happy woman. Through business, her husband had befriended Andrew Carnegie, then the richest man in America. Since Carnegie had no sons, he offered to take Tom Arthur (James' third son) out to Pittsburg and put him to business there. Mrs Arthur would have none of it. She declared that her son was "not going to a godless country". The boy stayed at home!

In this political cartoon of 1873, Mrs Arthur, the first woman to be elected to a male-dominated school board, is presented to her worried and distraught male colleagues.

In 1873, Jane Arthur was elected a member of the first Paisley School Board. It was to be noted that she was the first female to hold such an appointment. She was said to have a refining influence on the male dominated board and was esteemed by all. After her election to this austere body, "it was whispered that the lady shows sometimes an inclination to espouse the cause of shrieking sisterhood who rave about women's rights!" It appears that Jane Arthur was an early pioneer of women's liberation!

Like her husband, Jane Arthur was a generous benefactor to worthy causes. This "Lady Bountiful" espoused the fight against strong drink in Paisley. One example of this was her gift of the"Cabmans' Rest" in County Square. Erected in 1877, this little building provided Paisley cabbies with a retreat where non-alcoholic drinks were served. She earnestly hoped that her gift would improve matters, as cabbies were noted at that time for "nipping in for a quick one" between customer calls!

Mrs Arthur was a frequent visitor to Quarrier's Homes in Bridge of Weir. A number of the orphans had expressed to her a desire to go to sea when they became older. In 1887, the generous lady gave £3,000 to the homes. The donation was used to build a training ship on dry land, to train the orphans in seamanship. The ship, the "James Arthur," was a fully-rigged brig with double-top sails. It had full working gear and was provisioned as if going on a foreign voyage!

Many hospitals benefited from her interest. To compliment her husband's gift of the ground to build the West Kilbride Convalescent Home, Jane Arthur instituted a fund to pay for the patients' care. She provided clothing for the convalescents and even helped them to re-establish themselves in their own homes. In Paisley, the inmates of Craw Road Hospital were provided with daily meals, paid for by the Arthur family.

The 'Cabmans' Rest' in the middle of County Square was donated by Mrs Arthur in 1877. It supplied non-alcoholic drinks in the hope that the drunken cabbies would make use of it, instead of 'nipping in for a quick one'.

Arthur Street in Paisley's West End was named after this "angel" of the hospital wards. Her husband gave money to build a men's "Model Lodging House" in this street. Mrs Arthur always took a great interest in the welfare of its occupants. For nearly a century many men were grateful for its shelter.

Always interested in medical matters, she, gently and wisely, made efforts to improve the lot of patient care in hospitals. By 1896, she had become the president of Paisley Infirmary Hospital Guild.

In 1892, she combined her pet causes of medicine and the advancement of women when she founded a bursary for women medical students at Queen Margaret College, Glasgow University. This enabled women to graduate in medicine there for the first time.

Jane Arthur out lived her husband by seventeen years and continued to be a kindly, generous lady. She left Barshaw to spend the last three years of her life at Ayr. The funeral of Paisley's "Lady Bountiful" took place from Barshaw House in 1907. She lies buried in the family vault at Woodside. Her husband's statue, stands sentinel over the precinct of Glasgow Cathedral, a reminder of his generosity to many causes. James, her grandson, sold Barshaw Estate to the town in 1911 and the park opened to the public in 1912. Mrs Arthur would have been pleased to know that her home continued to shelter those in need, first as a home for Belgian refugees and wounded soldiers during the Great War, then a maternity hospital and latterly an old folk's home. And, of course, hundreds of Paisley Buddies still enjoy a day at Barshaw Park.

Ferguslie Park

Ferguslie Park mansion house in its days of glory.

Ferguslie Park House, which became Glen-Coats Hospital was, without doubt, one of the most magnificent mansion houses, not only in Paisley, but in Scotland. Today, nothing of it remains but the name which lives on in the surrounding housing scheme of today, Ferguslie Park.

Its owner, Thomas Coats, later to be Sir Thomas Glen-Coats, was the son of Thomas Coats of Ferguslie, the thread magnate and mill owner. In the 1870s, Thomas Coats Snr. had purchased the site of an old tower house, known locally as Ferguslie Castle, and had held this land in trust for his son. In 1876, young Thomas decided to build a splendid new residence to welcome to Paisley his Montreal-born bride, Elize Agnes Walker. The house, which he called Ferguslie Park, was initially a medium-sized building, built in the Baronial style. When the newly-weds arrived at their new house, what a welcome they received. At the entrance to the estate, Ferguslie mill workers had erected an archway with a motto made of roses saying "Welcome Home". On another part of the estate, an arch was built wishing the couple "Health and Happiness". Even the master bedroom had a painting of Cupid, with his arrow aimed at the newly weds!

By the late 1880s, however, the house had become too small for a man of such high social standing as Thomas Coats, who, as a mill owner's son, was expected to lavishly entertain high class guests at his home. Hyppolyte Blanc, a Belgian architect based in Edinburgh, was commissioned to built a massive enlargement to Thomas' home. Blanc was an architect who had served

Sir Thomas Glen-Coats. *Lady Glen-Coats*

members of the Coats family well. He had just finished the design of St James Church in Underwood Road for Sir Peter Coats. By 1890, the greatly enlarged house at Ferguslie was completed. There was much to admire in the very high quality work, notably the carved detail of the dormers and the Jacobean and French Rococo interiors. The house cost, then, the massive sum of £50,000 and was a mixture of Scottish and French Renaissance styles. It was a little palace, built for a merchant prince of Paisley.

Soon, accolades came to the proud owner of Ferguslie Park. In 1894, he was created a Baronet, with the title of Sir Thomas Glen-Coats. As a staunch Liberal, he was elected MP for Paisley from 1906-10. After this, he did not seek re- election. In 1908, he was appointed Lord Lieutenant of Renfrewshire. After the election hustings of 1926, when Asquith stood as Liberal candidate for Paisley, a reception was held at Ferguslie Park. The main guests were Lord and Lady Asquith, Lloyd George and his daughter Megan, and Lady Bonham Carter. Asquith described the house as a "typical millionaire's villa, with some Corots, a Sir Joshua Reynolds, and a Hoppner intermixed with family photographs and some sentimental mezzotints".

Garden parties were often held at the house. To celebrate the declaration of peace in the South African War, Lady Glen-Coats entertained the families of soldiers and sailors who had been involved in the war. Luckily, a huge marquee had been set up on the lawn for her guests, as that day there was a torrential rainstorm. A bountiful tea was served and various presentations made, when the rain ceased and the guests were able to stroll around and admire the beauty of the estate and buildings. As the guests left, mothers were given a gift of tea, and children a bag of sweets. All received a parting handshake from their kind host and hostess, Sir Thomas and Lady Glen-Coats.

As an honorary Colonel in the A & S Highlanders, Thomas Glen-Coats sits in the centre beside the officers of that regiment. The picture was taken at a recruiting campaign in the grounds of Ferguslie House in 1915, during the dark days of WWI.

In 1910, the house was further extended by local architect, T.G. Abercrombie, who enlarged the library wing and created a very grand billiard room.

During the Great War, Thomas Glen-Coats who was an Honorary Colonel in the Argyll and Sutherland Highlanders acted as a recruiting officer for local soldiers. It was said that new recruits "were paraded at Ferguslie Park in deep snow and were kept shivering for two hours", because the out-of-town commanding officer could not find his way to the house!

Thomas Glen-Coats died at Ferguslie Park in 1923, as the result of an accident. The house devolved to his son, Major Harold Glen-Coats, who, in turn, bequeathed it to the Royal Alexandria Infirmary in 1933, to be used as an auxiliary convalescent hospital. It became known as the Glen-Coats Hospital and functioned successfully for many years. One local annual event, eagerly looked forward to, was a garden fete held in the hospital grounds in aid of hospital funds. In 1946, a special 'V' for Victory and Thanksgiving fete was celebrated. There were stalls for flowers and plants, gifts and books, a milk and ice cream bar, lucky dips and home baking. There were even two palmists to tell one's fortune! In addition, there was "tricky turf bowling', dancing displays, processions, band contests and a health and beauty display. The grounds that day must have been a happy sight, with Paisley people letting their hair down after the war was won.

Sadly, this fine mansion was demolished in 1982.

James Arthur of Barshaw

*Portrait of James Arthur
of Barshaw and Carlung.*

If Paisley Buddies fail to close a door behind them, they are often asked, "Were you born in a park?". Their pat answer is, "Yes. Barshaw !". Hundreds of Paisley men and women first saw the light of day when Barshaw House was used as the Burgh maternity hospital, the first of its type in Scotland.

A house has stood in the lands of Barshaw since 1695. Successive owners from that time have been William Macdowall, Robert Smith and William Brand. In 1858, the house and estate was bought by James Arthur, who paid Brand the, then enormous, sum of £9,000.

James Arthur was born at Arthurlie, near Paisley, in 1819. His family ran a weaving and bleaching business in Foxbar. Having learned all about the cloth trade, young James decided to become a draper. He borrowed £100 and opened his first draper's shop in Paisley High Street, in 1837, living above the shop. Always keen to watch over his business, James set up an ingenious means of communication between his home and shop. He installed a speaking tube through the floor! His business prospered.

It was when purchasing stock in Glasgow, that he first met Hugh Fraser, then a lace buyer and later manager of Stewart and McDonald, a Glasgow warehouse. Hugh Fraser decided to leave this firm to set up a partnership with James Arthur and, in 1849, the new partners started business as retail drapers, in Glasgow's Buchanan Street. The firm was a great success.

Seeing a gap in the market, James Arthur opened up a wholesale business, in which he could supply shops throughout the land with his goods. Business also boomed from this warehouse in Argyle Street. Within a few years, James Arthur and Hugh Fraser went their separate ways. Fraser became a retailer and established the House of Fraser, while Arthur, in 1856, founded Arthur & Co. a wholesaler and manufacturer of drapery.

Between 1856 and 1876, James Arthur continued to expand his business into the largest of its type in Scotland. Branches were opened up in England and Ireland and James Arthur became a very wealthy man.

View of Barshaw House in its original splendour.

Sometime between 1856 and 1861, Arthur enlarged the late 18th Century mansion of Barshaw, by adding a substantial west wing. Further extensions were made in the 1880s, including a magnificent, cast-iron,"bird-cage" conservatory. The local architect, John Hutchison, designed the new work in the, then fashionable, Italianate style.

Arthur was described as "a brusque, undersized figure, broad as to the shoulders, burly in the paunch and firmly set on the legs. A-top of all is a bullet shaped head: with a face, keen and not very cultivated, but humourous withal and bearing, above everything, the look of one accustomed to give orders, and see that they are carried into practice". Other contemporaries thought of him as "an admirable man with a vigorous physique, untiring energy, rapid decisions, sound judgement and fearless courage".

James Arthur was a generous benefactor to the town of Paisley. In 1863, he donated money towards the building of a new Grammar School at Oakshaw. In 1871, he gave funds for the purchase of books for Paisley's new library and made liberal donations to Paisley Infirmary, of which he was a director. For the needy of the town, he gave the Model Lodging House in Arthur Street.

In 1877, he purchased 'Carlung', an estate near West Kilbride, which became his favourite country retreat. It was here that he died in 1885. At the time of his death, his personal estate was worth some £1,049,000.

In 1888, the 'Crown Window' in the west gable of Paisley Abbey was dedicated to James Arthur and, in 1893, a statue was erected in Glasgow's Cathedral Square, to honour this merchant prince of Paisley. Arthur's grandson, James, inherited Barshaw Estate. This was sold to Paisley Burgh in 1911, becoming a public park in 1912. A model yacht pond was opened in 1924 and Barshaw Golf Course one year later.

The official opening ceremony of Barshaw Golf Course took place in 1926.
Provost John Glover addresses the crowd in pouring rain!
(photo courtesy Paisley Museum).

Wee boys and grown men have been sailing their model yachts in the pond since 1924

During the Great War, Barshaw House was given over to Belgian refugees and used as a convalescent home for wounded soldiers. From 1921, the house was used as a maternity hospital, finally closing its doors in 1959. The old mansion house then became a geriatric hospital and lasted as such until the early 1990s. James Arthur would have been pleased to know that his old house had been put to good use over the years and is now a listed building, presently restored to its former glory.

Provost Peter Eadie

Portrait of Peter Eadie, one of Paisley's most popular provosts. (1905-8)

In 1839, when Peter Eadie was two years old, his family came to stay at Williamsburgh in the East end of Paisley. His father, a well-educated stone mason, had obtained much needed work in helping to build the new railway station at Paisley Gilmour Street.

When this work was completed in 1840, Peter's father became unemployed. Poverty, fever and smallpox afflicted the family. For a time, it even looked as if Peter's mother and father would be 'destroyed along with their chicks'.

However, they survived and young Peter was sent to Lawn Street Infant School. When his father managed to get employment in a local brewery, the family moved to Thread Street. Peter now went to Seedhill School, where he was often in trouble. On one occasion, he was the ringleader in a stone-throwing battle with the rival Thread St School. During the battle, Peter managed to break several school windows. His poor parents had to pay for damages which they could ill afford. Ironically, Peter was later transferred to the very school he had damaged. He found there that" life was so hard and bare".

To supplement the family income, Peter was sent to work as a shop messenger boy. On one occasion, the mischievous boy was late in returning to the shop. He and his friend decided that, rather than face the irate shopkeeper, they would run away to sea. They headed for Glasgow, but ended up in Stirling! Needless to say he lost that job.

His forgiving father got his wayward son a job in the brewery, where Peter became "chief bottler", filling 300 dozen bottles a day. The trouble was that he kept sampling the ale at the same time! The brewery manager thought Peter was a "disgrace to his works" and dismissed him.

Next, he became an apprentice mechanic with Robert Kerr, one of Paisley's leading shawl makers. Part of his work included hammering in rows of nails into a block of wood. But the way Peter wielded the hammer caused the shop blacksmith some concern. He angrily shouted to Peter,"Dae ye think it's razors yer makin?"

119

Peter Eadie carefully tends his Ring Traveller machines at his workshop in High Street. (photo courtesy Eadie Bros).

In 1853, Peter joined Blackwood and Gordon, the high-class shipbuilders in Paisley, to finish his apprenticeship. When this was completed, he was told to go, as "there wis nae work for the Yaird".

During this time, Peter spent his social Saturday nights with his friends. They sang religious songs and read poetry and formed a society "The Paisley Harmonic Association". At one of their evening meetings, a girl stole Peter's "very best silk handkerchief". Peter reciprocated by taking her bible. He then wrote some poetry and hid it in the bible, hoping to meet up with the girl in question. However, another girl, a Miss Riddle, saw the poetry. She was amazed that such a serious poem had come from the pen of this "rattleskull o' a daft laddie". They later married and Peter settled down in his ways.

He was now an engineer and worked on Clyde steamers in Glasgow and locomotives in Kilmarnock. In 1863, he returned to Paisley, where he worked for Hanna, Donald and Wilson. He was sent to erect gas holders in Scotland, Ireland and on the Continent. In 1867, he went to Galashiels to erect a gas holder. He saw a job vacancy with a local textile engineer, R & A Sanderson, and joined the company.

Registered trade mark for Eadie's Ring Travellers

During the next three years, he secretly experimented in his Galashiels kitchen, designing a small machine to produce 'ring travellers'. These were small, but crucial, components needed in textile spinning machines. By 1872, Peter's little sideline was beginning to flourish. Samples were sent to Paisley's gigantic thread mills at Anchor and Ferguslie, where, after trial and error, they became a great success.

Peter Eadie returned to Paisley the same year and set up business in a machine shop in the High Street. There, he worked slowly yet steadily, making so many travellers, without once stopping for a break. The family were astonished that the once harem-scarem Peter was now a successful, hard-working family man. He even became interested in local politics, upholding the radical Paisley tradition and working for "the humbler classes".

Peter's company expanded greatly and, in 1896, moved to a new purpose-built factory complex in the East End of Paisley, not far from Williamsburgh where the poor Eadie family had first settled in Paisley.

When Peter Eadie was made Provost of Paisley in 1905, it was said that "although he was not born with a silver spoon in his mouth, he could now sup with one if he so wished". He died in 1919, leaving two legacies. One was his firm, Eadie Bros & Co Ltd and their famous "ring travellers", which still travel across the world today. The other was his great-grandson, the politician, Tony Benn.

W.D.McLennan

W.D.McLennan (1872-1940) (Photo courtesy Prof F. Walker).

In the 1960s and 70s, many of Paisley's old buildings were demolished in the name of progress, but some gems of architecture remain for Paisley people to admire. Foremost among them are the works of a Paisley architect, William Daniel McLennan. McLennan was one of Scotland's most original architect/designers during the first quarter of the 20th Century.

He was born in a tenement in Glen Street in 1872. His father, Tom, came from a weaving family and first worked as shawl designer in Paisley and then became a shawl manufacturer, establishing a family business. William, his son grew up in a world of texture, colour and design. The family prospered and built a detached villa in Carriagehill.

Young William attended the John Neilson Institution, where he proved to be a bright pupil, winning the Peter Brough Bursary three times. In 1889. he left school and enrolled in the Government School of Design in Gilmour Street (Paisley's art school). His studies completed, it is thought that he served his apprenticeship with Peter Caldwell, a local architect, working on buildings for the Paisley Co-operative Society. In 1896, after a brief spell in Ireland, Mclennan returned to his native town and set up his practice in the Masonic Buildings, High Street.

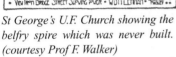

St George's U.F. Church showing the belfry spire which was never built. (courtesy Prof F. Walker)

The magnificent Art-Nouveau interior of St. George's U.F. Church.

Readers may fondly remember one of his first designs, the elegant bandstand in Brodie Park. It was a favourite Sunday outing to go to hear music in the park and, in its heyday, the bandstand attracted popular entertainers. Sir Harry Lauder and Dame Nellie Melba once played gramophone records to the crowds!

McLennan had a liking for half-timbered, Tudor buildings. He was also influenced by the current Art Nouveau style of his Glasgow contemporaries, among them Charles Rennie Mackintosh although the two never met.

These influences helped develop his unique style and his masterpiece, now called St Matthew's Church, in Gordon Street is a monument to his talent. The church was built between 1905 and 1907 with funds raised by the congregation. The red sandstone building was designed on a cathedral plan with nave, aisle, transept and chancel. Although basically Gothic, the Art Nouveau influence can be seen both inside and out. A massive belfry spire was originally planned, but lack of funds prevented this being built. McLennan was an elder in the church and presented it with four communion cups. He became furious when the church decided to remove his carefully designed wrought-iron work from the chancel to allow a better view of a new memorial window!

The Bull Inn in New Street also shows that, like Mackintosh, W.D. McLennan planned every little detail of his buildings. The interior of the pub shows his mastery of layout and delightful use of stained glass. Since 1901, the Bull Inn has kept its charm and unique character and is much loved by Paisley Buddies (especially for its steak pies!)

McLennan designed this splendid shop and tearoom in 1899. His client was Gibson, the baker. Of all the Paisley tearooms in the High Street this proved the most popular. Alas, it was demolished to make way for a modern Woolworth building.

Around this time, McLennan designed large villas in Thornly Park. Later in his career, he became more interested in architectural engineering and accepted less domestic work. In the last fifteen years of his life, his only commission in Paisley was "Thorscrag", a large villa at the edge of the Braes. Made of concrete with the appearance of sandstone, it displays his mastery of design, engineering and the 'new' technology.

Little is known of William McLennan's personal life. One of his acquaintances remembered him as a quiet man, who enjoyed a game of cards and a 'wee dram' in the evening. He wore a wide-brimmed hat and a bow tie and was often seen driving through the streets of Paisley in his open-topped Lanchester car. He remained unmarried and died in 1940.

This Paisley man is now beginning to be recognised as one of Scotland's most original architects. His best work, St Matthew's Church, is among the finest Art Nouveau buildings in the country.

When McLennan's Tudor half-timber design for Watson's butcher shop appeared at the top of New Street in 1900, it must have turned a few heads. Sadly the building is long gone.

The Bull Inn, New Street, shows McLennan's mastery of space and delightful use of light and stained glass.

Archibald Barr F.R.S.

Sketch of Archibald Barr. (1855-1931) Inventor of the rangefinder and height finders for anti-aircraft gunnery.

In the field of inventions which changed the world, the name of a Paisley man stands out. He designed and made a small optical instrument, the range finder. This invention was to change the course of modern warfare, the nature of naval and land artillery and the design of cameras and binoculars. The inventor's name was Archibald Barr.

Archibald Barr was born at Glenfield House, Castlehead, Paisley, on 18th November 1855, third son to a local yarn merchant. After a classical education at Paisley Grammar School, Barr served an engineering apprenticeship at the large, local works, A.F. Craig. He studied part-time at Glasgow University and was one of the first to graduate with a B.Sc. in engineering, in 1876.

Barr continued at this university for eight years, working as an engineering assistant to Prof. James Thomson, elder brother of Lord Kelvin. In 1884, Barr gained his doctorate and was appointed to the chair of engineering at Yorkshire College, Leeds, later to become the University of Leeds. It was here that Prof. Barr established the first engineering research laboratories in Great Britain.

In 1888, while at Leeds, Prof. Barr noticed an advert in the "Engineering" publication, inviting proposals for a single-observer rangefinder. Barr and his university colleague, Prof. Stroud who was head of physics, collaborated on a prototype.

In 1891, officials from the War Office went on board HMS Arethusa to observe the rangefinder in action. Barr and Stroud were delighted to show that using their rangefinder enabled the gunners to aim at their target with accuracy. The design more than met the brief set by the government. Barr commented "the result was emphatically in our favour".

Prior to this, in 1890, Barr had been recalled to Glasgow University, to be appointed Regius Professor of engineering and mechanics. This was distinction indeed, as it was the oldest such university chair in the world. At Glasgow, Barr had freedom in pursuing his private research. At Leeds, the university authorities had objected to their mechanics working on Barr's rangefinders!

In 1899, Barr & Stroud opened a factory ar 44 Ashton Lane, Glasgow. Five years later the firm moved to Anniesland Cross. The firm is now based in Govan.

Archibald Barr acted as Guarantor for the 1911 Glasgow Exhibition. It was due to his enthusiasm for anything mechanical that motor cars made an appearance there.

Barr settled in Glasgow and set up his house at Dowanhill. Here, he assembled his first orders but, as orders increased, he opened a small workshop above the entrance to Hillhead Subway Station. The firm, Barr & Stroud was established. Soon, their rangefinder's reputation had spread as far as Japan and was even copied by the famous, German optical firm Zeiss! By 1904, Barr & Stroud had moved to a three-storey factory at Anniesland, such was the international demand for their products.

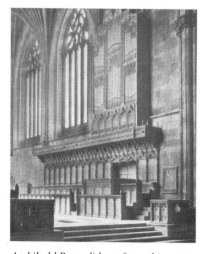

Archibald Barr did not forget his native Paisley. In 1929, he anonymously donated a large sum of money towards the cost of the organ in Paisley Abbey.

Despite the pressures of a fast growing business, Barr still devoted a lot of time to Glasgow University. His outstanding achievement was in founding the "James Watt" research laboratories, the first such resource for the engineering faculty. These were opened in 1902 by Lord Kelvin and were hailed as the most comprehensive in Britain. In 1913, due to pressure of business, Barr retired from his university post. During the Great War, Barr & Stroud had bulging order books and their instruments greatly contributed to the war effort.

For his pioneering work and invention of the rangefinder, Barr was given the highest accolade in British science. In 1923, he was elected a Fellow of the Royal Society.

Barr, although a distinguished scientist, inventor and ingenious mechanical engineer, became quite a 'character' as he grew older. In his office at Anniesland, he shared a very large desk with his partner Stroud. They sat facing each other. Cigars helped Dr Stroud concentrate, while Barr liked sugar-coated doughnuts. Each day, a bag of them was put in his desk drawer and, when deep in thought, he would open the drawer and munch his way through his delectable doughnuts. If their staff came into the room and found the air thick with smoke and Dr Barr's drooping moustache covered with sugar, they would realise the partners had been dreaming up new ideas.

Barr held other important posts such as President of the Royal Philosophical Society and acted as Guarantor for the 1911 Glasgow Exhibition. He was a founder member of the Scottish Aeronautical Society and promoter of the memorable Lanark aviation meeting in 1910.

In such a busy life, he did not forget his native Paisley. In 1929, he donated a large sum of money towards the new organ in the choir of Paisley Abbey. He died in 1931,

Barr designed and made a small optical instrument, the range finder. This invention was to change the course of modern warfare, the nature of naval and land artillery and the design of cameras and binoculars.

Kenneth MacKenzie Clark

Portrait of Kenneth MacKenzie Clark.

In the thread-making dynasty, Clarks of Paisley, one member stands out, not for his love of the family business, but for his love of the good life. His name was Kenneth MacKenzie Clark.

He was born in Paisley in 1868. His father was James Clark, who, shortly before the birth of his son, had been the sole owner of Clark & Co Thread Mills in Paisley. Young Kenneth, as befitting the son of a wealthy mill owner, was sent to be privately educated at John Graham's School in Greenock. However, the ivory towers of academia had little appeal to the adventurous Kenneth. Instead of completing his education, he left school at fourteen to accompany one of his older brothers on a trip to Australia and New Zealand. While in New Zealand, the unconventional Kenneth stayed in a Maori village, where his prowess as a billiard player impressed the Maori Chief. So much so, that he was offered the chief's daughter as a bride! But, being a proper, young, Paisley gentleman, Kenneth declined the offer.

As a young man back in Paisley, Kenneth had been taught all the pastimes thought appropriate to the son of a wealthy mill owner. He had spent most of his evenings honing his skills at snooker and billiards, a game which entranced him. He was encouraged to take up yachting by his uncle John, who owned several first-class yachts. Sailing large yachts was the privilege of the rich, industrial families of the West of Scotland and the Clarks of Paisley were no exception. In later years, Kenneth would own and sail several yachts like the 'Katoomba' and the 'Kariad', the latter an eighty-foot boat in which he competed against members of his arch-rivals in trade, the Coats Family.

In 1890, Kenneth was recalled to Paisley, to join his uncles, Stewart and John Clark as a director in the family mills. He was 22 years old. His first duty was to travel with a delegation of local thread manufacturers to St Petersburg, to negotiate the sale of thread to Russia. The trip was a huge success.

On his return to Paisley, Kenneth and his uncles set about another more important sale. This time, the buyers were their old rivals Messrs J & P Coats. Negotiations dragged on between the Clarks and Coats for many years.

Among the several first class yachts Kenneth's Uncle John owned was the celebrated 'Vanduara', the pride of Paisley.

The town of Paisley watched with bated breath while rumours and speculation ruled the day. Finally, in 1896, an agreement was reached and the two companies joined forces. The new company was the largest of its kind in the world.

Kenneth Clark and the remaining co-director, his uncle Stewart, had sold the family interest for a whacking two and a half million pounds! Shortly after the amalgamation of the two businesses, Kenneth lost interest in the thread business. His maxim in life was "If business interferes with your pleasure, give up business." This he did. He intended to enjoy his new found wealth. By 1900, he had acquired a town house in London's salubrious Grosvenor Square, a mansion in Perthshire and two large yachts. That same year he also acquired a wife, when he married his cousin, Alice McArthur.

John Clark encouraged his nephew Kenneth to take up yachting,

In 1904, when the opportunity arose to buy Sudbourne Hall, an 18th century mansion with eleven thousand acres of the best shooting ground in Surrey, Kenneth jumped at the chance. He had the house converted by his architect in the 'rich style'. No expense was spared. The house's fifty fine rooms were sumptuously decorated . Guests marvelled when they saw acres of the best oriental carpets, Adam fireplaces, marbled sculptures and the grand staircase decorated with 250 pillars.

Part of the Anchor Mill complex, once owned by Kenneth Clark and his uncle Stewart Clark.

Kenneth enjoyed acting as host to a large circle of friends. He held lavish parties when he would entertain his guests with conjuring tricks. Rabbits would appear out of hats and guests' watches would be 'eaten'. His only child, also Kenneth, thought "he was the best fun in the world."

When the summer season came round, the family and its entourage of servants would leave to spend their holiday at the fashionable resort of Mentone on the French Riviera. Kenneth was fond of a gamble and would spend a considerable time at the casino in Monte-Carlo. He became celebrated as "The Man Who Broke the Bank at Monte Carlo". In fact, he broke the casino bank several times!

However, Kenneth Clark was no social climber. When he was offered a title by Lloyd George, his reply was "Go to hell!" Kenneth MacKenzie Clark was his own man and slightly eccentric. Unfortunately, he was over-fond of a dram and this was ultimately to be his downfall. He became severely ill. His last days were spent on one of his estates at Ardamuchan Peninsula. He died there in 1932, aged 64.

His only son and heir was Sir Kenneth Clark, the world famous art-historian. He said of his father's and his two Clark uncles' drinking habits, "The whisky bottle claimed them all".

Robert Broom

Robert Broom devoted his life to discovering early mammal-like reptiles of the African continent. Broom's important finds shifted science's search for early man from Europe to Africa. (Photo courtesy Transvaal Museum).

Two Paisley men have been honoured on postage stamps. William Notman, photographer, Canada and Dr Robert Broom, paleontologist, South Africa.

Half of Paisley has never heard of the latter. Who was this son of Paisley who made the 'Big Time' unearthing the early history of mankind? Who was the man who considered" no one to be his superior, and very few his equal"?

Robert Broom was born at 66 Back Sneddon Street, on 30th November 1866. He was the third child of John Broom and Agnes Hunter Shearer. His father was a shawl and calico print designer employed by Forbes and Company in Paisley.

Robert spent his summer holidays with his grandparents at Millport. There he was to be seen combing the beach for different forms of marine life which he avidly collected. It was on this beach that he first encountered an old retired veteran soldier, Major Leavach, who, in earlier days, had fought along with Wellington in the Peninsular Campaign. Leavach encouraged the little six year old boy in his study of marine biology. Their friendship never dwindled over the years .Years later, Broom was to discover and name a fossil after his old friend.

Dr Robert Broom holding his beloved skull of "Australopithecus".
(Photo courtesy Transvaal Museum).

At the age of nine, Broom first studied botany. By the time he was eleven, he could name every genus and species of flower to be found in Scotland. Broom was educated at Hutcheson's Grammar School, Glasgow. When he was sixteen, he became junior assistant to the Professor of Chemistry at the University of Glasgow, and studied under Lord Kelvin. There he graduated Bachelor of Science as a twenty-year old. Two years later, he graduated as a Doctor of Medicine and Surgery.

After practising as a Doctor in Australia for several years, Broom moved to South Africa in 1897. Although a successful physician, Broom always maintained a strong interest in palaeontology and comparative anatomy. He became Professor of Zoology and Geology at Victoria College from 1903 until 1910, but, becoming restless with city life, Broom took off to explore the Karroo Desert region, where he prospected for fossils. Here he found fossils of early mammal-like forms which he meticulously catalogued and classified. This early work in documenting the transition of reptiles to mammals, gave him an honoured position in the annals of science. In 1928 he was awarded the Medal of the Royal Society for his brilliant work.

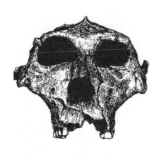

"Australopithecus".

In 1925, Broom heard that the first early fossil hominid had been discovered in a limestone quarry near Kimberley, by his friend Ramond Dart, a South African anatomist. Broom was overjoyed. Dart never forgot how Broom burst into his laboratory unannounced and ignoring him and his staff, strode over to the skull and dropped to his knees "in adoration of our ancestor". He supported Dart 's view that this skull represented an early ancestor of man. In 1933, Broom published a book entitled "The Coming of Man". In 1934, he was appointed paleontologist to Transvaal Museum.

Broom lost no time and set about exploring limestone quarries in the Transvaal. He was extremely successful in his quest and, in a few years had amassed new examples of early hominids and allied groups from a number of sites. Broom's richest site, discovered in 1936, was at Sterk-fontein where he discovered a complete adult skull, some fragments, a complete pelvis and parts of long bones. What he was first to discover were the remains of "Homo Erectus", the first man to walk upright a million years ago. His findings were published in "Nature" in 1936.

What a discovery to make at the age of 69! In 1938, he heard that some teeth had been unearthed by a schoolboy near this site. After invading the local classroom. Broom bought the teeth from the boy for a few shillings, throwing in five chocolate bars for good measure. The boy then led him to the cave, where he had found the teeth. Here Broom found the remains of a robust form of Australopithecine.

British scientists, notably Sir Arthur Keith, refused to accept the large body of evidence that Broom and Dart had gathered in respect of early man and regarded them as South African renegades. Richard Owen, Director of the British Museum, Broom's scientific mentor, thought highly of his talent. However, had he lived long enough, Owen, who hated Darwin and his Theory of Evolution, would have been appalled that Broom's discoveries supported the theories of his rival!

Broom did not forget his Paisley ancestry and made one last trip to his native town where he was presented to the Provost. At the same time, he was honoured at Glasgow University.

In 1950, Broom wrote another book "The Missing Link" which summarised his life's work on human ancestry. He died a year later. His contemporaries described this Paisley man as a "brilliant, eccentric Scot" who, over forty years, changed the course of the search for early mankind to Africa. Broom triumphed and lived to see "Piltdown Man" exposed as a forgery and his own work established as a landmark in the search for human origins.

The Paisley Police

The 1936 annual inspection of Paisley Burgh Police Force in the Drill Hall.

Paisley formed its first law-keeping force as early as 1661. The town, at this time, was guarded by four town officers by day and at night by a small number of night watchmen. The night watchmen were town inhabitants who turned out on a rota system. For a time, their duties were performed with great enthusiasm and dedication as they walked Paisley's dark, unlit streets to preserve the peace. However, over the years, those whose turn it was to keep guard at night often sent in substitutes, any number of whom could be hired for a small payment.

By 1792, this practice was frowned upon and soon remedied by the introduction of hefty fines on the offenders. Three years later and again in 1800, to augment the force of policemen, a number of respectable gentlemen were appointed as special constables, armed with batons. All 500 of them!

When the Police Act came into force in 1806, it divided the town into two distinct police 'beats'-the old burgh on one side of the River Cart and the Newtown on the other. For many years, the two forces had their own separate commissioners, courts and police stations. The Newtown police station was no more than a small front shop. Prisoners were confined there in a small back room with a heavily-barred window. The Burgh beat used the town Tolbooth as its headquarters and jail. In later years, as the town grew, the two forces merged.

Paisley Burgh Police badge.

Throughout the town, sentry-like, wooden boxes were erected, offering primitive shelter to the night watchmen. One of the watchmen's duties was to call out the hours during the night, when most of the town's inhabitants were in deep, nocturnal slumber. Many towns people were rudely   awakened by the stentorian shouts of these night watchmen.

In 1806, the police force consisted of a superintendent, two sergeants, four corporals, a clerk, a surveyor of houses and twelve night watchmen. The night watchmen worked long hours, in summer from 10pm-5am and in winter from 9pm-6am. The police beat extended one mile in every direction beyond the burgh boundaries. This allowed capture of criminals fleeing outwith the town.

Criminals apprehended by this small police force faced some peculiar modes of punishment. It was common practice to banish law-breakers beyond the burgh boundaries. On one occasion, two women were released from the Tolbooth Jail at Paisley Cross. Wattie Peacock, the town drummer, then led the women at the head of a procession towards the town's boundaries. As they reached the old bridge near the Cross , large crowds had gathered to pursue the two women, who made frantic efforts to distance their tormentors. They escaped the hostile crowd by finding sanctuary in the house of a good Samaritan, fleeing the town when night fell.

Joining the burgh police force in Victorian times was easy. A man with a good physique was considered a good candidate. The physical test for entry was quite undemanding. A quick, visual inspection of his naked body was made to check for deformities. If none were found, he was well on his way to becoming a policeman. In addition to this, he had to pass a moral and literacy test. All that was required of him was to write out the Lord's prayer in a legible hand. New recruits were obtained mainly from the labouring classes of big, strapping Highlanders and Irishmen, who solemnly took the oath "to guard, to watch and patrol" the narrow wynds and streets of the Burgh of Paisley.

Over the years, various Police Acts came into being and were adopted in Paisley. Local Police Bye Laws followed and supplemented these acts. Paisley, in 1892, was a busy market town and it was no surprise that specific laws were made concerning cattle droving through its main thoroughfares.

Paisley Police Burgh HQ in Gilmour Street lay behind the arched entrance adjoining the old burgh buildings. It must have been one of the few police stations to have such a large jail nearby!

"No person shall drive any drove of oxen, cows or heifers between the hours of 9am and 11pm". The number in a herd was not to exceed 36. This included "any wild, dangerous or infuriated animals"! Billiard halls in the town were not permitted to have any disorderly conduct or to suffer persons of bad character! In Paisley's public parks, no person was to bathe, wade or wash in any pond or fountain. Drivers of Hackney carriages must be able to read or write, be of good character, experienced in driving, be free of infirmity of body and mind and be cleanly in person and wear a good hat!

In the 20th century, all the neighbouring burgh police forces merged to become Renfrew County Constabulary. It, in turn, joined with Paisley Burgh Police. In 1975, all became part of Strathclyde Police. Older readers will remember the hilarious scenes at Paisley Cross during the 50's, when cattle regularly made daring escapes from Storrie Street market. As the poor beast ran down the busy High Street, it was often pursued by a perspiring policeman who had lost his hat in the chase! Perhaps readers will also remember calling into the police headquarters in Gilmour Street Jail to report the loss of an escaped pet budgie. Ah! These were the days!

Lewis Fry Richardson F.R.S.

Lewis Fry Richardson FRS. Principal of Paisley Technical College and School of Art between 1929-1940 remembered as "A man before his time".
(photo courtesy University of Paisley).

When the eminent scientist Lewis Fry Richardson was appointed Principal of Paisley Technical College in 1929, he took up his official residence in a large house at Castlehead.

After converting part of the house to a laboratory, his top priority lay in securing all his scientific papers, some as yet unpublished, in the house safe. Above the safe he painted a large sign, THIS SAFE IS NOT LOCKED. This, thought Lewis, would protect his papers from fire, while deterring any burglar from blowing the safe and destroying his years of personal research.

Up to this time, he had published around 66 scientific papers, including an epic book, "Weather Prediction by Numerical Process". This, written when he was superintendent of Eskdalemuir Weather Station, described the mathematical technique of weather forecasting. The trouble was, in 1922 when the book was first published, it took Lewis about three months and 100,000 calculations to give a forecast for the following day! No computers then!

As a result of his brilliant pioneering scientific work, mainly in weather prediction, Lewis Richardson received international acclaim. He was elected a Fellow of The Royal Society in 1926, Britain's highest scientific honour.

On a pleasant summer's day in 1930, a lanky figure, dressed in green corduroy, rode his bicycle along Paisley's Canal Street. As he passed a lady, he raised his Panama hat with such vigour that his bicycle wobbled dangerously. This was Richardson, the archetypal eccentric professor! However, when he dismounted at the George Street entrance to the college, the janitor greeted him with great respect. After all, to have such an eminent scientist in charge at Paisley was a rarity. He had specially come to college on a Saturday to make measurements for his honours class in physics, such was his dedication to his students.

As Principal, he was expected to work at the college from 9am-10pm during weekdays, giving lectures to students for 16 hours a week. He also had to run the college administration. Despite his heavy duties, he conscientiously cared for his students. In a letter to a student he wrote, "As you weren't present yesterday evening, I write to correct a mistake in my lecture of 23rd..."

'Dunscore', Main Road, Castlehead, where Richardson converted part of the house to a research laboratory.

Saturdays and Sundays gave him time to work on his latest private research-the mathematical study of wars and their prevention. As a life long Quaker, Richardson abhorred war. He had served as an ambulance driver in the First World War and seen its horrors. In the late 1930s, he redoubled his efforts to complete his war studies and alert the public to the likelihood of another conflict with Germany, before it was too late. In 1939, he visited Danzig before its invasion by the Germans. The Paisley Daily Express published his observations.

When war broke out, he gave a series of lectures to the A.R.P. in Paisley, highlighting the dangers of gas attacks. As he spoke in highly technical terms beyond their understanding, his audience must have regarded him as a crank!

On one occasion, Richardson invited all the neighbours to his house at Castlehead, to discuss air raid precautions. The hum of conversation drowned out Richardson's several efforts to get the meeting underway. Suddenly, there was a crash! Everybody turned round to see the speaker flat on his back. "That, ladies and gentlemen, is the correct procedure in the event you hear a bomb dropping. We will now begin the meeting".

Lewis Richardson and his wife Dorothy were both air raid wardens during the war. One night, a bomb landed about 250 yards from their house.

Lewis raced to the scene and noticed no damage had been done. He saw a woman standing in the dark, on the far side of the bomb crater. He called out, "Go away you stupid woman-a bomb has exploded!" Her reply was, "Don't shout at me-go away yourself!" "I am a warden, so do as I say", shouted Lewis. The woman replied, "I am also a warden-you must be Lewis". It was, of course, Dorothy!.

On a more light-hearted occasion, Lewis' nephew, the celebrated actor Ralph Richardson, appeared in a play at Paisley Theatre. His uncle, always the practical joker, sat in the front row making faces in an attempt to make his nephew forget his lines!

Richardson was a keep-fit fanatic and often jogged past the gates of Paisley's Anchor Mills. The mill girls would dance in a line behind him, calling out in friendly banter. Little did they realise that this eccentric figure was a famous scientist.

Lewis Richardson pioneered a new type of geometric measurement, later developed by Mandelbrot, now called "fractals". He is now known as the "Father of weather prediction". Buildings are called after him at the Met office HQ in Bracknell and at the University of Paisley. There is also the Richardson Peace Institute at the University of Lancaster. He was remembered at the "Richardson Lectures" held in his honour at The University of Paisley, as part of their centenary celebrations, an event which even Richardson could not have predicted!

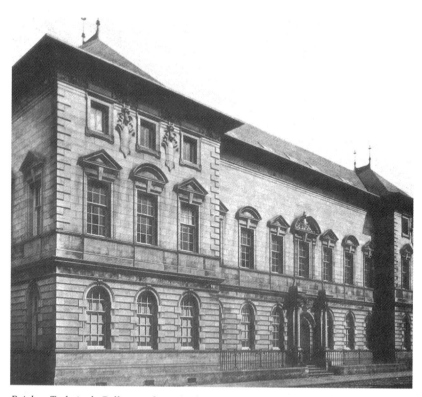

Paisley Technical College, where Richardson gave up many of his weekends to experiment in physics.

Willie Telfer-"Mr St Mirren"

St Mirren F.C. 1948 on the hallowed turf at Love Street. Willie Telfer proudly stands in the back row, third from right.

"Give me a good centre-half and I will build a team around him", were the prophetic words of Bobby Rankin, manager of St Mirren F.C. Rankin found his man in 1943, when he signed Willie Telfer, a young man from Larkhall who worked in a local slaughterhouse.

Willie Telfer was a product of that famous nursery of Scottish football, Burnbank Athletic. He was first spotted by a Ranger's scout, when playing for this team in 1941. The scout was impressed and the following Saturday Telfer was to be given a trial at Ibrox. The thought of playing at Ibrox made the talented, young seventeen year old a nervous wreck and, for a whole week before the biggest game of his life, he hardly slept a wink. As he took the field he trembled and, during the game, his play was abysmal. Needless to say he was not signed by Rangers. However, the St Mirren scouts kept an eye on the young player and, two years later, he signed for the Paisley team.

Over the next fourteen years of his football career, Telfer would play a pivotal role at Love Street. He was tall, strong, dominating and resourceful and he quickly made his mark on the team. The team manager, Bobby Rankin, moved Telfer from his usual right-back position to centre-forward. In this new position, Telfer soon hit the headlines in the local press. The Buddies loved him. Paisley fans were convinced that this was the best switch the manager had ever made.

Telfer keeping his eye on the opposition.

Telfer had a steadying influence on his colleagues in the St Mirren defence. It was claimed that Telfer never broke sweat. He didn't have to, as few defenders could read a game better than him. Rarely was he lured out of position and rarely could forwards get past him.

The modest Telfer said of his game, "I just stayed on my beat. I knew my job was simply to stop the player coming through the middle". He became so popular with the Love Street crowd, from the Caledonia end to Carter's Corner, that he was dubbed "Mr St Mirren".

Curiously, in season 1947-8, Telfer was the one and only centre-half on the team's books. The manager thought a reserve player for Telfer's pivotal position unnecessary!

Telfer was now one of the best players in Britain and was knocking on the international door. However, he was denied many Scottish caps as one player got in his way. Big Geordie Young of Glasgow Rangers was Scotland's first choice and Telfer rarely got a look in.

Although Telfer was finally capped against Wales in 1954, he was best known as one of the greatest clubman in Scotland. He was a cool, calm centre-half, who helped St Mirren out of trouble in many a game.

Telfer was a loyal St Mirren man. In his fourteen years at the club, he had only asked for a transfer three times. In 1954, Fulham FC, who had never seen him play, were keen to get him for £12,000, but, in typical Paisley fashion, his club wanted £17,000 to release him so the deal fell through. These were considered huge transfer sums at that time.

Willie Telfer affectionately called "Mr St Mirren" by local supporters. He was surprised, in the twilight of his career, to play for Glasgow Rangers. When his boyhood dream came true, he uttered these words, "Gosh I'm a Ger at last!"

Then, in November, 1957, headlines appeared in the national press. "Rangers sign new centre-half." When the Paisley Buddies read their newspapers they were shocked. The new centre-forward for Rangers was no less than their Willie Telfer! The transfer shook the football world and certainly shook Telfer himself.

The deal had been kept a closely guarded secret. The first Telfer knew of it was during his normal training session one evening at Love Street. He was told by the coach to go and see the manager, but it was nothing important. As Telfer got to the manager's office, he was told that there was a club interested in him. Would he like a transfer? Telfer pondered, thinking it was just another English club. He replied that he had no wish to go to England. Then, Willie Reid, the manager, laughed, "It's not an English club , Willie. It's Rangers!" Telfer nearly fell through the floor. Fifteen minutes later, Reid and Telfer were at Ibrox to sign the forms.

The transfer was controversial. Rangers supporters argued that Telfer was past it at the age of thirty. How could he replace the great Geordie Young, who had retired from Ibrox? And, if Rangers supporters were startled at the transfer, St Mirren fans were furious that "Hauf oor team" had been allowed to leave the sacred turf of Love Street. Protest meetings were held in Paisley and there was even talk of boycotting the club. Insults were thrown at St Mirren Directors, whose only reply was that, "The fans should consider it an honour for Telfer to join Ibrox. It's a great step up for him." The Paisley fans were not convinced. What would their team do without Willie Telfer? Over the years he had been an institution in the town.

Although Willie Telfer was as surprised as anyone at his sensational signing, deep down in his heart he was delighted. His boyhood dream of playing for Glasgow Rangers had come true. At Ibrox, Telfer continued to be as confident and imperturbable as he had been with St Mirren. The Rangers fans were won over and the veteran of thirty years became the hero of Ibrox.

Christmas in the 40's

Behind the tall gates, the snow-clad scene shows the old Albion Street Industrial School, home of the poor neglected children of Victorian Paisley.
We can only wonder what kind of Christmas Day they spent in such an institution.

Christmas celebrations in Paisley in the late 1940s, compared to today, was a 'dreich' affair. For a start, the town had no public Christmas illuminations. Only a few churches had outside coloured lights adorning their Christmas trees. Only a small number houses displayed 'fairy lights' in their windows and most of these had been bought before the war. Most working class families could ill afford such an expensive luxury and anyway, they had the terrible habit as soon as they were draped over the tree of going 'phut'! However, some enterprising fathers, entering into the spirit of Christmas, placed a hand coloured ordinary light bulb below the tree to light it from below. Trees were usually placed at the parlour window and sat in a bucket of well-watered soil scraped up from the back court. Although Christmas trees could be readily purchased in local shops, someone always knew somebody who could acquire a tree for 'free'. This was typical Paisley!

A Victorian Christmas card dated 1868.
(courtesy D. Malcolm)

Just before the Christmas school holidays, most primary pupils spent their last few days at school making decorations to take home. These were 'paper chains' made from sticky strips of coloured paper in blue, red or yellow, stuck together in loops. Making 'Chinese' lanterns to hang on the Christmas tree was another favourite.

Most pupils attended the obligatory Sunday School Christmas party dressed in their best clothes. The girls in party dresses the boys in kilts. After a quick tuck in of lemonade and crisps and home made cakes the tables were cleared. The floors of the church halls then took a pounding as the children played traditional party games. These ranged from dances such as 'strip the willow' when most boys and girls became lost in a tangle of moving bodies to "The Grand Old Duke of York" when you had to kiss your partner as you quickly dived under a human archway. Blind man's buff was a tame affair compared to "Bee Baw Babbity". All went well in this game until you had to stand isolated in the middle of a circle and were forced to chose a partner of the opposite sex after the singing had stopped. This usually entailed a quick, sometimes embarrassing. kiss.

The highlight of the party was the entrance of Santa Claus. If it was a posh church, a donkey usually accompanied Santa. The donkey usually got more attention than Santa, that is, until he opened his sack of presents. The biggest disappointment was not in the presents he handed out but his strangely familiar footwear. His 'give away' Wellington boots might have come from any High Street shoe shop! And anyway what had happened to the reindeer that we had all read about in books and seen on Christmas cards?

Back home the Christmas day lunch usually ended up being served at tea time since most Paisley fathers worked on Christmas day. To a Paisley, still suffering from the shortages of a recent war, with food rationing still on the cards, the main course on the menu was the trusty steak pie, served from an enamel ashet. The pie had to be ordered from the local butcher about one week before Christmas. Usually a small deposit secured the order and the ashet had to be returned after Christmas, in good order, to the butcher to get back the deposit.

In 1909 this snow -clad winter scene of Coats Memorial Church was painted by the Paisley artist Robert Sivell. (courtesy Paisley Museum)

Turkey was off the menu for most Paisley people as it was then considered a luxury. However, if the family taste in food extended to rabbit or ironically, reindeer at Christmas there was no shortage. These could be seen limply hanging on hooks outside butchers shops in Moss Street or High Street. The weather was usually so cold that the carcasses were frozen anyway!

The Christmas weather in 1947 produced snow so deep in the streets of Paisley that a small boy could easily fall down and literally disappear in drifts over two feet deep. The River Cart was frozen over. It was so cold that you could skate along Glasgow Road not to the ice rink, but to Barshaw Pond for a free skate! Some of the young 'posh' boys from Ralston made the 'parkie's life a misery at Barshaw. They would lift the park benches over the ice to the middle of the pond during the night, just before a thaw. The poor park keeper, up to his waist in water the following morning had the job of fishing them out!

In one of the coldest winters ever, coal was in short supply due to a miner's strike. Not to be out done, the people of Paisley kept the home fires alight over the Christmas and New Year period by burning wooden bobbins. These were supplied and bought from Paisley's vast thread mills by the sackful, to supplement what little coal was available. Coals from Newcastle should have read...from Paisley!

The writer leaves you with a song written by Mrs Fulton of the Glen. This is the song she sang to her three month old daughter, Alice, at Christmas.

"Oh ! Santa Claus,
It's time your toys were ready,
Feel in your pockets, sir,
If you've got any cash;
For I hope you'll bring some pretty thing,
To this wee bonnie leddie;
Oh! I trust you'll remember
Every wee bit lad and lass."

The Paisley tenement

Back court of two-storey, rubble built tenement with turret stair, built around 1820 at 8 Barr Street to house four families. The brick toilet block on the right is a much later addition. Property condemned in 1954 as being overcrowded and having a low sanitary category. Demolished soon afterwards. Notice the housewife emerging from the back close carrying a white enamel pail, like "Mrs Pail o' Wattir" of Dunn Street fame.

Many a famous Buddie was born and brought up in a Paisley tenement. Kenyon Wright, one of the brains behind the new Scottish Parliament, first saw the light in a tenement in Dunn Street. Kenneth McKellar, Scotland's ambassador of song, was born in a tenement in Mary Street. Archibald McKellar Paisley's ace Battle of Britain pilot, first started life in a sandstone tenement in Southpark Drive, now marked by a plaque. Hector Nicol, comedian, hailed from Howard Street.

Paisley is rich in tenement buildings of all shapes and sizes and in all quarters of the town. An astonishing variety displays itself, from the 'stone cliffs' of the High Street to the sloped splendour of Causeyside. Who could ignore the elegant sweep of red sandstone buildings in McKerrell Street, where each facade of the tenement wall is adorned with the most beautiful intricate stone carvings.

The elegant sweep of the red sandstone tenements in McKerrell Street in Paisley's East End, built at the turn of the century. Each building has its own unique set of intricate stone carvings beneath the elegant bow windows.

To have been brought up in a Paisley tenement did not imply poverty. It was the home of all classes of people. The only social distinction, if there was any, was whether you lived in a 'wally close' or not. The wally close was a source of inordinate pride to those privileged to dwell in it and houses in a building with a wally close usually had inside toilets. However, more often than not, most tenement dwellers in Paisley had to make do with a toilet on the 'stair-heid' landing. There, ensconced in a small cubicle sat the W.C., with its well-worn wooden seat and high level cistern operated by a chain pull. This toilet was shared with other families on the same landing. The wee room had no electric lighting, no heating and was freezing in winter. Squares of newspaper were carefully threaded on a string and hung from the cistern pipe to serve as toilet paper. The inside face of the wooden door sometimes bore the carved initials of previous tenants.

What all the tenements had in common was the brick wash house built in the corner of the back court. It contained large wooden sinks, a circular copper boiler and a large wringer. In the 'wash-hoose', the Paisley housewife did the family's washing on her allocated day. Some women even washed their family in the boiler! A favourite trick of local boys, the terrors of washing day, was to set fire to the elasticated rubber contents of a golf ball and drop the smouldering rubber down the wash house chimney. They would quickly disappear, leaving the poor housewife to suffer the acrid smell of this home-made stink bomb.

Some back courts were well-maintained and sported green lawns and colourful flower beds. Others had no grass at all. It had disappeared over the generations, with boys digging holes to make 'mugs' for the game of marbles. The only signs of digging in some back courts was a hole to bury the family "budgie"!

In the streets, the tenements presented a sea of glass windows. Cricket was played on the pavement using a real leather ball and wickets were chalked on the bottom of the lamp standards. Hitting a 'six' usually ended with a broken window and the sudden departure of the whole team into nearby closes! To claim the ball back from an irate housewife was out of the question. In any case, another ball could easily be 'acquired' from Kelburne or Ferguslie Cricket Clubs.

During the summer holidays from school, the tenement streets became one long playground. It was safe then to play in the streets. In Dunn Street, for example, there were only two cars parked. One belonged to a taxi driver, the other to a doctor.

'Peevers', was a favourite game played by both boys and girls. Pavements were decorated in coloured chalks, the 'aeroplane bed' being the most difficult to set out. This was usually done by an older child with a good command of geometry. To have a 'peever' made from a flat piece of marble was considered the 'bees knees', but most children had to content themselves with an old shoe-polish tin. Other games enjoyed in tenement life were 'kick the can', 'hunch cuddy hunch' (a form of leap frog against the tenement wall), 'statues' and 'film stars'.

Some closes were declared out of bounds to children and running through them had their punishments. In one such close in Dunn Street, a housewife known by the name of "Mrs Pail o' Wattir", drowned her intruders with the contents of her trusty, white enamel pail.

Every tenement in every street in Paisley had its gangs of marauding boys. Candidates wanting to join one of the gangs in the East End of the town, whose shared territory stretched from Clarence Street to Kilnside Road, had to pass an initiation test. To a small boy of five or six the test was quite daunting. The object was to climb the complete length of a series of high dykes between the back of McKerrell Street and Kilnside Road. These walls, the highest that could be found in the area, appeared to the small boys as insurmountable as Everest. This stretch of wall was known locally as the 'gents'. The name came into being because the Abbey Manse, occupied by Rev Dr Gentles, once stood nearby the Glasgow Road end of the wall. So the phrase "to do the gents", came into being. Only the tallest boys succeeded, many came to grief because they were too small.

Tenement life in the forties and fifties in Paisley was a good preparation for later life and life long friendships were made. To 'come up oor close' was always a significant feature of Paisley social life. The close was a continual hive of activity. It was immaculately swept, washed and decorated in white pipeclay by the hardworking women. It was a place to meet and talk with your neighbours or shelter from a sudden shower. During Hitler's war, a time of gas masks and shrapnel and baffle walls, the close was a place to shelter from air raids. Nowadays, door entry systems prevail and children run no longer run through the closes, with the street as their playground.

The Fifties in Paisley

Paisley Cross in the 50s, with tramcars, buses and shoppers galore.
Burton's corner on the left was the favourite stance of 'Wee Dougie' the newsvendor.

Paisley in the 1950s had a buzz about it. In those days, Paisley had full employment, a plethora of light and heavy industries, shipyards, giant thread mills, tram cars, steam trains and Young's buses! Its shopping centre had a style of its own. A stranger would know he had arrived in Paisley.

Paisley's busy streets were still alive with the town's best known characters. Ta Ta Bella could be seen in tenement back courts, performing his unique song and dance act to the delight of local children. Flannel Jaws was a noted "coo pelter" or cattle drover, who was often seen at Storie Street Cattle market. The red flannel he wore over his head and tied beneath his chin gave him his nickname. His appearance resembled Vincent Van Gogh after he had cut off part of his ear. Like the Pied Piper of Hamlin, crowds of young boys would follow him through the town.

Going round house doors selling bundles of sticks was the occupation of Johnny Firelighter. On one occasion, he arrived at the lodge of Spiersfield House and knocked at the front door. When the housewife appeared, he asked her if she wanted to buy his firewood. When she declined the offer, Johnny

Paisley Cross in 1951, a seething mass of Saturday shoppers and football crowds.

Firelighter made his way to the back door, naively thinking that he had arrived at another house. Needless to say, the same housewife opened the door. Johnny Firelighter, not recognising the woman he had just spoken to a moment before, said, "See that wumman roun' the corner, she didna want any firewood. Dae you?"

One of the town's favourite characters was Wee Dougie, who could be seen regularly at Paisley Cross selling newspapers from his stance. Dougie Goodwin was very small in stature and had been, at one time, a circus clown and theatre entertainer.

He became well known in Scottish Music Halls, acting as the ventriloquist's dummy to Johnnie Beattie. He made many appearances at Paisley Theatre.

Another newspaper vendor who stood at Paisley Cross was a character called Ha' Pa 'Two. He was totally illiterate and could not even tell the time from the Town Hall clock. His customers kept asking him for the time, causing him no end of embarrassment. To overcome his difficulty, he once asked a customer to tell him the time. The reply was "Half-past two! ". For the next forty years, this character stood at the Cross, hoping some of his customers would ask him the time. Whenever he was asked the time, he would reply, "Ha' Pa' Two!"

And who could forget Cuthbert, dressed in a yellow oil-skin with a bright yellow sou'wester over his ruddy, weatherbeaten face. In one hand he held a walking stick and in the other hand a poke of sweeties and a small leather purse. This purse was rarely opened, thanks to the charitable, local shopkeepers.

Paisley High Street 1951, viewed from the top of New Street.

The author remembers him queuing in Mr Bain's fish shop in Kilnside Road. As he was served, Cuthbert would ask for two slice of filleted sole, the dearest fish in the shop. When it came to paying for the items, Cuthbert would carefully show his purse and say, "How much is that Mr Bain?" Mr Bain, with a shrug of the shoulders, would say, "It's all right, Cuthbert." and kindly send him on his way. Cuthbert's favourite joke was to tell a child that there was a hole in his sock. When no hole was found, Cuthbert would reply with a beaming smile, "Yes there is. The hole that you put your foot through to get them on!" Paisley people quickly learned that, if you entered a conversation with Cuthbert, one of the first things he would ask was where you stayed. If you did divulge your address, you might find Cuthbert on your doorstep the next day!

In the fifties, Paisley could boast eight large cinemas. To the young folks of the town, Hollywood was the big-time place and an all-American culture prevailed. Juke-boxes appeared in various cafes, notably in the Silver Lounge next to the Regal Cinema. In Causeyside, Cardosi's cafe became a mecca for the young people of Paisley. There they would enjoy American soft drinks, milk-shakes and Espresso coffee served in glass cups. Cardosi's was the place to be seen. All of Paisley's future talent gathered at Cardosi's. John Byrne the painter and playwright turned his early memories of the cafe into a movie. John Reid, who was part of the social scene in Cardosi's, became heavily involved in the music world, ending up as manager to Elton John.

Before they finished their evenings in the cafes, young lads would spent many hours at the "Monaco,"the fancy name for the Working Men's Abstainer's Club at Orr Square. Over the billiard and snooker tables, many a Paisley 'hustler' gambled his week's wages on the green baize!

Storie Street Baths would also be 'hotching' with young people on hot summer evenings, especially on mixed bathing nights! At the ice rink, Paisley Pirates reigned supreme and Moss Street on a Saturday became a seething mass of football supporters heading for Love Street.

In the fifties, Paisley was the place to be!

The Dummy Railway

The photograph, taken in the late 1960s, shows a specially laid on steam enthusiasts train crossing Lacy Street near its junction with Cyril Street. This was the last passenger train to use this line. The brick building on the left formed part of the Linside Laundry. (photo courtesy Paisley Museum).

A passenger train crossing the "Dummy Railway" was a rare sight indeed!

Less rare was the occasional freight train drawn by a rusty old steam engine dubbed "Puffing Billy" by the children in the East end of Paisley. With such few trains running, this suburban railway became known in Paisley patois as the "Dummy Railway".

The photograph, taken in the late 1960s, shows a specially laid on steam enthusiasts train crossing Lacy Street near its junction with Cyril Street. This was the last passenger train to use this line.

The train has just left the low level depot of John Lyon coal merchant. The brick building on the left formed part of the Linside Laundry, Cyril Street. It was owned by Messrs. Gibson and Reid, art dyers, French cleaners and carpet beaters. Only in Paisley could your "French" be cleaned up with a carpet beater all in the same shop! In the background is the Gothic spire of Sherwood Church.

In the 1940s, the same scene repeated itself; a rusty old freight train, trundling slowly over Lacy street; anxious pupils heading for Williamsburgh School trying to cross the line, trying not to be late. However, if he had simply "slept in", a street-wise pupil could always blame the train!

The special passenger train had stopped briefly underneath the Arkleston footbridge. Steam enthusiasts were having a great day! (photo courtesy Paisley Museum).

The train had its blessings. It once carried a huge pile of American G.I. helmets. These were off-loaded in Lyon's scrap yard. All the boys in nearby Dunn Street helped themselves to the G.I. helmets, not long after the days of gas masks, shrapnel and baffle walls The slight rust on the helmets was of no consequence. Perhaps it was an indication that they were battle-scarred. After all, what boy would miss an opportunity like this, a few helmets missing, from what seemed like a mountain. This was our way of getting a piece of the action from good old Uncle Sam.

Local legend has it that during WWII the train carried on board an anti-aircraft gun.During air -raids the old train would rush up and down the line with gun at the ready. No hits were recorded!

Sometimes pupils, for a prank, would place halfpenny coins on the line as 'Puffing Billy' slowly thundered towards them. The coins were ironed out to penny size and then 'squeezed' in to penny chewing chum machines in the neighbourhood, much to the chagrin of local shopkeepers.

The history of this railway was short. Opened in 1897 as part of the Paisley/Barrhead Railway suburban network and built at great expense over difficult topography, it soon made a loss. Despite this loss, it was bought by the Caledonian Railway in 1902 who hoped to "exploit the riches of Gleniffer Braes" and sustain a nexus with the growing prosperity of Barrhead. Alas for the promoters of this railway, in the same year the Paisley tramway system became electrified, offering a cheaper, more convenient mode of transport. So it was that the line became known as the "Dummy Railway with little or no public patronage.

Another stop on this, the last passenger trip on the old line, took place at Hawkhead Station. The pretty little station like the 'Dummy Railway', has disappeared from the scene. (photo courtesy Paisley Museum).

The few exceptions however, were during WWI when the occasional train carrying wounded soldiers and sailors could be seen crossing over the high level railway at Lacy Street and disembarking at Paisley East Station (the former site of the Kelburne Cinema). The wounded were then transported by road to Ralston House, requisitioned as a Red Cross Hospital, where it was hoped the men would recover. Paisley East Station was eventually demolished just prior to 1933, together with the two viaducts over Glasgow Road and Lacy Street.

Gone forever are the sights and sounds of steam, the rusty rails, the hewing gum machines, the halfpenny, the penny, and of course the G.I. Helmets!

Crawford Fairbrother M.B.E.

Crawford FairbrotherM.B.E. 1936-1986.

When wee Paisley boys were naughty, their angry mothers might threaten, "You'll end up in the Kibble." Other mothers would scold their children and shout out, "You're for the high jump!" In one particular Paisley household, the latter words were to prove prophetic to the ears of the young Crawford Fairbrother.

Crawford William Fairbrother was born in Paisley on 1st December, 1936. His father had been, in his day, a top class high jumper who had been runner-up in 1928 and 1929 at the Scottish championships. So, early in life, Crawford followed in his father's high footsteps.

Crawford Fairbrother winning the three A's High Jump for the first time in 1959.
He soars over the bar using the 'straddle' technique of which he was the master.
(photo courtesy of H.W. Neale)

While a pupil in the John Neilson Institution, Crawford began to compete as a high jumper in the mid 1950s. Coached by his dedicated father, Crawford won the Scottish Schoolboys' High Jump event in 1955 by clearing 1.78 metres. Heartened by his first victory, he continued to compete. He was to prove that rare phenomenon, the brilliant schoolboy who would sustain his performance into adulthood. His natural talents were honed and perfected through his own highly disciplined efforts and constant training. Over the years under several coaches, he refined his technique to perfect the 'Straddle', one of the jumps used at that time.

In 1956, he came third in the Scottish Championships, clearing his own height of 1.87 metres. From that time onwards, Crawford Fairbrother was to dominate this event in Scotland for more than a decade and put together a record unsurpassed for the time. In 1957, he became the Scottish high jump champion and held the title for thirteen consecutive years, a remarkable achievement. In the Scottish context, Fairbrother broke all national records.

In 1959, he became the British three A's champion for the first time and the following year he became the first British athlete to clear 2.01 meters indoors. Crawford broke the British record twice more, when he again won the British and Scottish titles over the next two years. He had soared to an amazing height of 2.06 metres on both occasions!

Crawford Fairbrother was now the undisputed British Champion. He was honoured by Paisley Town Council with a civic reception in the Town Hall and presented with an inscribed silver salver to mark his great sporting achievement.

Crawford glides over the hurdles.
Easy for a high -jumper like him!

One incident which took place at London's White City Stadium in 1962 reflected the character of this redoubtable Paisley man. A cloudburst almost washed away the match between Great Britain and Poland when there was two inches of water lying at the high jump take off. Appropriately for a man who was by profession a meteorologist, Fairbrother was undaunted and proceeded to 'hammer' his Polish opponents. In drier circumstances, their personal best were some two or three inches higher than his own. It takes more than a little rain to put off a Paisley man!

Fairbrother was totally committed to his sport and self-discipline was the order of the day. He trained three times a week at Love Street with St Mirren F.C., lifted weights at Renfrew and practiced his high jumps at his Glasgow Victoria Park's Athletic Club. Despite his busy training schedules, he always found time for his wife and young family, for golf and cricket as recreation and for his loyal support of St Mirren F.C.

Fairbrother was 'capped' a record fifty-three times for his country. He was given the honour of acting as Scotland's team captain at the three Commonwealth Games between 1958 and 1970. His own highest placing was at the Kingston Commonwealth Games of 1966 when he was fourth, an honourable achievement.

In 1970, the Commonwealth Games were to be held in Edinburgh. Speculation in the Scottish press ran high as to who would captain and lead the Scottish team into Meadowbank Stadium. Crawford Fairbrother was the obvious choice. The press reported "Fairbrother, thirteen times Scottish high jumping champion, had captained the Scottish team in 1962, at Perth, Australia, and had made an admiral job of it". Fairbrother who had made more appearances for Great Britain than any other person was indeed made captain. When he led the Scottish team into Meadowbank Stadium, the roar that was heard might well have come from Hampden Park! Crawford Fairbrother was given the distinction of taking the Oath for all the competitors at these games. It was a fitting tribute for an illustrious athlete in the final years of his long career.

Sadly Crawford Fairbrother M.B E. died in 1986, at the young age of fifty. Paisley and Scotland may never see his like again.

Bibliography

Books:

The Paisley Shawl; The Paisley Thread: M. Blair

History of Paisley; Paisley Burns Club; Paisley Poets: R. Brown

From the Cottage to the Castle: Coats

A General Description of the Shire of Renfrew,1782: Crawfurd &Semple

Judicial Records of Renfrewshire; Vanduara: W. Hector

Lanark & Renfrew: W. Hamilton

Paisley Abbey: A.R. Howell

Sanitation in Paisley: W. Kelso

Songs, Ballads and Fragments of R.Tannahill: A.Laing

Yesterday's Paisley; Recollections of Paisley;

Coal Flowers; Paisley Since the War: D. Malcolm

Abbey & Town of Paisley: C. Mackie

The poetical work's of Wm. Motherwell: J. McConechy

History of Paisley: W.M. Metcalfe

History of Paisley; Life & Opinions of Arthur Sneddon: J. Parkhill

Memoir of James Fillans: J.Paterson

Views in Renfrewshire: P.A. Ramsey

Paisley in Old Picture Postcards: V. Reilly

Pictorial History of Paisley; Golden Threads: Silver Threads: D. Rowand

Old Families and Olden Times in Paisley; Tannahill's Songs and Poems;

Paisley's Townhouse; St. Mirin;

History of the Lairds of Glenfield: D. Semple

Science & Gossip: A. Stewart

Magazines:

The Paisley Magazine 1828

Renfrewshire Magazine 1846-7

The Paisley Portfolio 1895

Seestu Magazine 1880

Newspapers:

Paisley Advertiser; Paisley Herald; Paisley Journal; Renfrewshire Independent; Paisley Daily Express.

The Author

David Rowand is proud to be a Paisley Buddie. He has spent many years of his life on a personal crusade extolling the virtues of his native town......to anyone who will listen. His love of Paisley flows like the River Cart through the very heart of the town. Perhaps this love is inherited, since his Paisley forebears have lived and worked in Paisley since 1672. Rowan Street, in Paisley's South End, is called after an ancestor, Robert Rowan, well-known in his day as the Laird of Dovesland and Kilncroft.

His first book 'The Pictorial History of Paisley', published in 1993 is still a favourite with the Buddies. One writer reviewing the book for The Glasgow Herald said of the author, "He knows more about Paisley than there is to know." His second book 'Golden Threads' published in 1999, became an instant hit in the town. His third book 'Silver Threads', published in 2000, delighted the Paisley public.

In 1977, David was the moving force behind the founding of the Old Paisley Society and was its first president. Today, he is the president of the recently formed Renfrewshire Family History Society, Vice-president of the Bohemian Club and Vice-president of the Tannahill-Macdonald Club. David was educated at Williamsburgh, South and Camphill schools, then studied architecture at Glasgow School of Art. He was elected a Fellow of The Society of Antiquaries of Scotland in 1980. In November 2000, David was awarded the distinction of being made a Fellow of the University of Paisley for his unique contribution and research into Paisley's history.